ssemble
nd sing!

-ROM INCLUDES:

50 IMAGES

IUSIC SCORES

LYRICS

VOCALS

PIANO
OMPANIMENTS

OR AGES
7-11

■ SCHOLAS

CW01003194

Assemble and sing!

Resources for assemblies and collective acts of worship

Paul Noble and Stuart Watkinson

■ 21 new songs and
assemblies

■ 50 images provided
on CD-ROM

■ Includes audio versions of
musical accompaniments

Credits

Authors
Paul Noble
Stuart Watkinson

Development Editor
Kate Pedlar

Project Editor
Fabia Lewis

Editor
Kathleen McCully

Series Designer
Anna Oliwa

Cover Illustration
Janos Jantner/
Beehive Illustration

Illustrations
Shelagh Nicholas

CD developer
Footmark Media Ltd

Minimum specification
PC: Windows 2000 or higher
Processor: Pentium 2 (or equivalent) 400MHz
RAM: 128 Mb
CD-ROM drive: 48x

MAC: OSX
Processor: G3 400MHz
RAM: 128 Mb
CD-ROM drive: 48x

Speakers can affect the quality of the sound recordings. For optimum sound quality use speakers with the following specification:
Frequency response 60–20,000Hz
RMS: 1.8 Watts

Due to the nature of the web, the publisher cannot guarantee the content or links of any of the websites referred to. it is the responsibility of the reader to assess the suitability of websites.

Text © 2008 Paul Noble and Stuart Watkinson
© 2008 Scholastic Ltd

Designed using Adobe InDesign

Published by Scholastic Ltd
Villiers House
Clarendon Avenue
Leamington Spa
Warwickshire
CV32 5PR

www.scholastic.co.uk

Printed by Bell and Bain Ltd

1 2 3 4 5 6 7 8 9   8 9 0 1 2 3 4 5 6 7

British Library Cataloguing-in-Publication Data
A catalogue record for this book is available from the British Library.

ISBN 978-0439-94576-9

Acknowledgement
Crown copyright material is reproduced under the terms of the Click Use Licence.

Every effort has been made to trace copyright holders for the works reproduced in this book, and the publishers apologise for any inadvertent omissions.

Contents

Introduction

Half a century ago, writers of school assemblies would have felt pretty secure in working on the assumption that Britain was a Christian country. Now the population includes around two million British Muslims, plus Hindus, Jews, agnostics, atheists and others. The balance of faiths has certainly changed and continues to do so, with children from different faith backgrounds living cheek by jowl with each other and mostly attending the same schools.

The 1996 Education Act applies in this case.

> 'All pupils… at a maintained school… shall on each school day take part in an act of collective worship' [Section 385.1].

> 'The collective worship… shall be wholly or mainly of a broadly Christian character' [Section 386.2].

The main thrust of the law is clear: for cultural, historical, educational and, inevitably, political reasons, Christianity is to hold centre stage as far as acts of worship are concerned. Clearly creating primary assemblies that are both legal and workable is therefore something of a challenge, a challenge to which my musical collaborator in this project, Stuart Watkinson and I have tried to rise. We are both Christians, but you will know that this label can be applied to a whole range of people, from the dogmatic to the liberal. So I must therefore state further that we are practising Anglicans. You will have to make do with that, else I will have to

turn this book into one on theology. If I am honest (surely this is the place to be that), we were chiefly motivated to write this book by a delight in using words and making music, coupled with a lifelong passion for teaching. It was not about the money. Trust me, I'm a Christian.

Church schools may wish to make more explicit and develop further the ideas outlined under the Christian core heading, but with very few exceptions and hardly any adaptation, the assemblies can be used with multi-faith groups. Concern for each other, concern for the environment, remembrance – these are not the exclusive province of Christianity.

The songs

We have tried very hard not to 'write down' to children with words or with music. We wanted to write material that would stand on its own merit and would not embarrass an adult to sing. The first hymnal ever written exclusively for children (Divine Songs for Children, 1715) was by the great hymn writer Isaac Watts, who wrote in his preface that he wanted his writing to be at 'the level

■SCHOLASTIC
www.scholastic.co.uk

of the child's understanding' and yet, 'if possible, above contempt'. It is an aim that we find hard to take issue with. A number of worship songs in current wide use in primary schools have been written to a social agenda, although some argue – the compilers of the English Hymnal, for example – that the worship of God is a hymn's sole function and that concern for mankind should follow from this. We believe that both 'the worship of God' and 'caring about mankind' are integral to Christian belief and need not be kept in false isolation from each other in our hymn books.

Alternative hymns are suggested from the following books:

C&P *The Complete Come and Praise*, compiled by Geoffrey Marshall-Taylor with arrangements by Douglas Coombes (BBC Books)
NBC *The Novello Book of Carols*, compiled by William Llewellyn (Novello)
SOP *Songs of Praise* (OUP/BBC Books)
SRTY *Sing Round the Year*, Donald Swann (Bodley Head)
WCV *With Cheerful Voice, Hymns for Children* (A & C Black)

The assemblies

Every opportunity has been taken to indicate where the presenter might involve the children and encourage verbal interaction or even action. It is expected that the presenter will wish to make the assembly his or her own, sometimes picking up on a particular aspect and running with it to the exclusion of what is written down. So be it. To maximise the use of the songs and the assembly material, not only are alternative assembly themes suggested, but also some links with SEAL and PSHE are pointed out. There are also a few suggestions for ways of exploring the issues back in the classroom, should you wish to do so.

I have recommended one piece of music for playing while the children are assembling. Of course there will be many possible alternative tunes and I have listed some in the annotated index (pages 92–94), a list that could form the basis of a school music resource bank. The accompanying CD-ROM provides resources for supporting and enlivening these assemblies. Those schools without the services of a resident musician can, with a little practice, use the recorded accompaniment provided on the CD-ROM by Stuart. We are indebted to the young and talented Hannah Johnson from Chesterfield for providing the sung examples to help you when teaching the songs.

How to use the CD-ROM

The CD-ROM includes the following material:

■ lyrics of the songs in the book
■ scores, as printed in the book
■ audio files of the songs with vocals
■ audio files of piano accompaniments only
■ images to support the assemblies.

Menu screen

■ Click on the resource gallery of your choice to review the resources available under that theme.
■ Click on **All resources** to view all lyrics, image and audio files available on the CD.
■ Click on **Photocopiables** to view and print the photocopiable resources also provided in the book that accompanies this CD.
■ Click **Back to intro** to return to the opening screen.
■ Click **Quit** to exit the program.

Resource galleries

■ Click **Help** to find support on accessing and using images.
■ Click **Back to menu** to return to the Menu screen.
■ Click **Quit** to exit the program.

Viewing and printing images

Small versions of each image are shown on the resource galleries. Click and drag the slide bar to scroll through the images in the gallery, or click on the arrows to move the images frame by frame.
■ Click on an image to view the screen-size version of it.
■ There are two options for printing the image. **Print using Acrobat®** enables you to print a large copy of the image as a PDF file.

Simple print enables you to print the image without the need to use Adobe® Acrobat® Reader®.
■ To return to the gallery click **Back to resource gallery.**

Song lyrics and audio

Each resource gallery includes the song lyrics and music linked to the assemblies within that particular theme. The following icons are used on the gallery screens:

 Lyrics only are displayed on the slide.

 The first verse and chorus are displayed on the slide; the audio includes a vocalist singing the first verse and chorus to piano accompaniment.

The lyrics of the full song are displayed on the slide. The words scroll down in time to the piano accompaniment.

The words can be made bigger or smaller using the **Increase/Decrease text size** buttons at the top of the screen. The lyrics of all songs will be set at this size unless changed again.

Slideshow presentation

If you would like to present a number of resources as part of your assembly, without having to return to the gallery, you can create a slideshow.

In the gallery, click on the + tabs at the top of each image or song you would like to use.

■SCHOLASTIC
www.scholastic.co.uk

Assemble and sing! For ages 7-11

It is important that you click on the images in order; a number will appear on each tab to confirm the order. If you would like to change the order, click **Clear slideshow** and start again.

Once you have selected your images – up to a maximum of 20 – click **Play slideshow**. To move between slides in your slideshow click on the blue arrows either side of the screen.

You can end your slideshow presentation at any time by clicking on **Back to resource gallery**. Your slideshow selection will remain selected until you clear the slideshow or return to the menu screen.

Photocopiable resources

To view or print a photocopiable resources, click on the required title on the list and the page will open as a read-only page in Adobe® Acrobat®. In order to access these files you will need Adobe® Acrobat® Reader® installed on your computer.

To print the selected resource select **File** and then **Print**. Once you have printed the resource, minimise or close the Adobe® screen. This will take you back to the list of PDF files. To return to the Menu, click **Back**.

Windows NT users

If you use Windows NT you may see the following error message:

> 'The procedure entry point Porcess32First could not be located in the dynamic link library KERNEL32.dll'.

Click on **OK** and the CD will autorun with no further problems.

Windows Vista users

If you use Windows Vista you may see the following error message when quitting the CD:

> 'This program might not have installed correctly'.

This message can be ignored as the program is not designed to be installed.

Setting up your computer for optimal use

On opening, the CD will alert you if changes are needed in order to operate the CD at its optimal use. There are three changes you may be advised to make:

Viewing resources at their maximum screen size

To see images at their maximum screen size, your screen display needs to be set to 800x 600 pixels. In order to adjust your screen you will need to **Quit** the program.

If using a PC, open the **Control Panel**, select **Display** and then Setting. Adjust the **Desktop Area** to 800 x 600 pixels. Click on **OK** and then restart the program. If using a Mac, from the Apple menu select **Control Panels** and then **Monitors** to adjust the screen size.

Technical support

For all technical support queries, please phone Scholastic Customer Services on 0845 603 9091.

Food for all

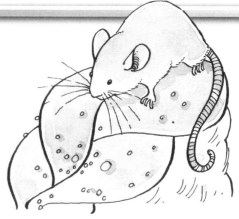

Christian core

Christians thank God for the world and all God's gifts, especially at harvest time, but Christian duty to the hungry and needy is clear (Mark 12: 29–31) that those with plenty can and should share with those in need.

Other key ideas

There is plenty of food in the world. Some countries produce more food than they need and increasing numbers of people in wealthy countries eat too much. Yet malnutrition is a huge problem and today we have the largest number of hungry humans in history. Most malnutrition is caused by the action of people (by conflict, terrorism, corruption, poverty and environmental degradation). We can do something about these things.

Music for assembling

Frederick Delius, *To Be Sung on a Summer Night on the Water 1* (2' 16"). *(Refer to Index for alternative suggestions.)*

Song on the CD

'O praise God for the harvest' has an easy range and should be sung brightly. The last verse can be used if the assembly is one where harvest gifts are offered up by the children.

See photocopiable pages 50 and 51.

Alternative music for singing

■ 'The Earth is yours, O God' by Michael Saward (*C&P*, 6). This is an eminently singable hymn with direct comprehensible lyrics appropriate to the assembly theme.

■ 'For the beauty of the Earth' by Folliott Pierpoint (*SOP*, 222; *WCV*, 23; *C&P*, 11). The fine words of this hymn have made it popular with singers and composers alike; consequently there are a number of good tunes to choose from. The traditional 'England's lane' is still the favourite, especially with the full harmonies in *SOP*. A more comfortable key is given in *C&P*.

Resources

Grains of wheat and a bag of flour or alternatively use seeds. Appropriate images from the CD include 'Harvest festival' and 'Drought'.

Presentation

In my hand I have something more precious than gold. What is it?

Show the wheat grains (produce the bag of flour as a clue). Describe the connection between what grows in the fields and what enters our stomachs. Show the 'Harvest festival' image.

Why is this more precious than gold? It is food, and without food we would all die.

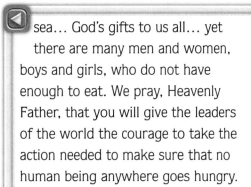

Give the children some information about the inequity of food supply (perhaps using the 'Drought' image from the CD from 'Moral and Christian teaching').

In this country, most people have plenty to eat and, in fact, one in five people eat too much and become obese. But many people in the world do not have enough to eat and a recent estimate (2006) gave this number as 800 million; 80 million are malnourished in China and people die daily of hunger in parts of Africa. The UN has said that in ten years' time, there will still be 412 million people with very low food intake levels. It is a fact that more people go hungry today than ever before in the history of the world.

Why is this?

You may encourage the children to contribute at this point. Touch on some of the problems – food distribution, conflict, corruption, poverty, political unrest, water supply, environmental degradation and unfair trade rules. End by making the point that the problem is not a simple one but that most of the causes of undernourishment are man-made, and we can do something about these.

Reflection or prayer

All over the world, people gather a rich harvest of food from earth and

sea… God's gifts to us all… yet there are many men and women, boys and girls, who do not have enough to eat. We pray, Heavenly Father, that you will give the leaders of the world the courage to take the action needed to make sure that no human being anywhere goes hungry.

Teach us, we pray, the joy of sharing. Help us to care for the world so that it will continue to provide enough food for everyone to eat. Help us… who have plenty… to find ways of sharing fairly with those who do not have enough.

Alternative assembly topics
- Christian Aid Week;
- Healthy eating;
- Wasting food.

Development
- Ask children to write down the countries of origin of all the foods in their larders. Collate the information using a computer or wall map.
- *What are 'fair trade' foods?* Investigate in the local supermarket. Examine the difference between fair trade and free trade (contact Christian Aid for information).

Links
SEAL: Getting on and falling out (empathy).
PSHE: 2h. To recognise the role of voluntary groups; **3a.** To know what makes a healthy lifestyle; **4a.** To realise that their actions affect themselves and others.

For peace sake

Christian core

Christianity is a faith of sacrifice and love, not war. Jesus said, 'Blessed are the peacemakers for they shall be called the children of God' (Matthew 5: 9), although Christians are exhorted to confront evil and 'Fight the good fight of faith' (Timothy 6: 12). We can give thanks for the sacrifice of those who gave their lives in war: 'Greater love hath no man than this, that a man lay down his life for his friends' (John 15: 13).

Other key ideas

Remembrance Day is about remembering the courage of those who suffered and died for their country. It is also about remembering the horror of war itself that, without Remembrance Day, we might forget.

Music for assembling

Edward Elgar, Variations on an Original Theme (Enigma), Op. 36 No. 9, 'Nimrod' (4' 11"). (*Refer to Index for alternative suggestions.*)

Song on the CD

'Children of your peace' is a hymn written specifically for Remembrance Day. Keep the melody moving to avoid the song acquiring a saccharine edge. This song also includes a part for recorder.

See photocopiable pages 52 and 53.

Alternative music for singing

■ 'Shalom', traditional (Hebrew song, *C&P*, 141). The title is Hebrew for 'peace'. This can be sung unaccompanied or as a round.

■ 'Lead us heavenly Father, lead us' by James Edmeston (*WCV*, 56), to the tune 'Mannheim', is a traditional Victorian hymn that falls within the range of a primary child.

Resources

Appropriate images from the CD include: 'Field of poppies' and 'Somme cemetery'.

Presentation

Mud. The only problem I have ever had with mud was when my mum used to tell me off for bringing mud into the house on my shoes. Have you had that problem? I actually quite like mud. I like riding my bike through mud and making lovely skid marks. I like squelching through mud when I've got my Wellingtons on. I even like handling mud when it is a lovely clean piece of sticky clay because you can shape clay into all sorts of things. Mud doesn't look beautiful very often, but it can do. I have seen great mountains of mud that have been piled up by mechanical diggers alongside a new road, covered in beautiful red flowers. Can anyone guess what flowers they were?

Talk about the children's answers. Show the 'Field of poppies' image from the CD.

Poppies are amazing flowers. Their seeds lie sleeping in the soil until they are churned over and they are

SCHOLASTIC
www.scholastic.co.uk

Assemble and sing! For ages 7-11

exposed to light and warmth. Then they will burst into flower, even in the most unwelcoming heap of mud alongside roadworks! A Canadian army doctor, Major John McCrae, noticed this happening when he was fighting nearly 100 years ago in the First World War. It was such a horrible war – so many millions of soldiers died that people simply called it the Great War. During that war, vast numbers of shells exploded on the soil of northern France and Belgium (Flanders) where McCrae was fighting. These shells turned the soil over, again and again, so that no living thing could be seen – except the poppies.

One day in May 1915, John McCrae's best friend was killed by one of these shells and John had to bury him. Looking out across the desolate, muddy battlefield, he wrote a poem that began:

In Flanders fields the poppies blow
Between the crosses, row on row...

You could display the 'Somme cemetery' image here to illustrate how many soldiers were killed in the war.

Crosses and poppies – these two things were linked together, and ever since, people all over the world have worn poppies to remind them of the crosses that mark the graves of those killed in that war. Nowadays we wear them to remember those who have

suffered and died in all wars, for if we remember that suffering and sacrifice, we have a chance of stopping such things from happening again. For the sake of peace, we must remember.

Reflection or prayer

They shall not grow old, as we who
   are left grow old:
Age shall not weary them, nor the
   world condemn.
At the going down of the sun and in
   the morning
We will remember them.

Laurence Binyon (1869–1943)

Dear Heavenly Father, we pray for peace… peace in the world… peace in our town, peace in our homes, and peace in our hearts. Amen.

Alternative assembly topics
- United Nations;
- Local memorials;
- Charitable organisations.

Development
- Visit local war memorials, such as town monuments, memorial halls and parks.
- Make a 'peace memorial' display decorated with poppies, memories and prayers.
- Discuss where conflict continues today.

Links
SEAL: Getting on and falling out (empathy).
PSHE: 2f. To resolve differences.

A new baby

Christian core

One birth is particularly special to Christians: without the birth of Christ there would be no Christianity. Jesus preached a message founded upon a love for God and for each other, so his arrival on Earth is regarded as the 'good news' – the beginning of God's gospel (story) of hope and love. (The familiar events of the nativity are recounted in Luke 2: 1–19, although for the story of the wise men you must refer to Matthew 2.) Birth is also a much-used Christian metaphor for choosing to follow the teachings of Jesus. There is an account in John 3 of Jesus telling a Pharisee that he needed to be spiritually 'born again'. Because of this, some Christians refer to themselves as 'born again' Christians.

Other key ideas

A birth is a unique event, that's why we remember and celebrate our own 'birth' days. Although it is also a common event, births are always treated as special. Muslims whisper prayers into a baby's ears as soon as it is born and Christians have their babies 'christened' soon after birth.

Music for assembling

Frederick Delius, *La Calinda* (4' 32"). (*Refer to Index for alternative suggestions.*)

Song on the CD

'Born on a winter's night' celebrates Christ's birth, but also, in the last verse, the newborn everywhere. Traditionally, carols are not just for Christmas.

See photocopiable pages 54 and 55.

Alternative music for singing

■ 'Mary's child' by Geoffrey Ainger (*NBC*) is a gentle, rhythmic carol, published in a number of forms.

■ 'O little town of Bethlehem' by Phillips Brooks (*WCV*, 97). Of the traditional tunes, Forest Green by Ralph Vaughan Williams sits particularly nicely within a child's normal singing range. You do not need to sing all of the verses.

Resources

Appropriate images from the CD include: 'Birthday party' and 'Mother and baby'.

Presentation

Was anyone born today?

Start by having an interaction with the children about the answers to this question. Move on to underline the fact that we celebrate the anniversary of our births. Let any birthday children come forward and talk about their birthdays in the usual ways – they could compare

■SCHOLASTIC
www.scholastic.co.uk

Assemble and sing! For ages 7-11

their experiences with the 'Birthday party' image from the CD. Follow up with a discussion about the actual days they were born. What do children know about that event? You will elicit some information but you should enter into discussion with children about the reason they know so little. Show the 'Mother and baby' image from the CD and talk about the helplessness of babies and why they need love, care and attention; in particular, stress that they too were babies once. Birth, including theirs, is a little miracle, something to be celebrated. Link here to the miracle of Christ's birth.

Alternatively, you might do a short series of assemblies simply telling the story of Christ's birth – a sort of daily soap opera on a Christmas theme. Do not assume that children know all the details of the Christmas story.

Reflection or prayer

O Lord our God, we give thanks for the birth of Jesus. In all the excitement of Christmas, amidst all the decorations, food and presents, help us to remember Jesus' message of love for one another.

Babies are tiny, helpless creatures that need lots of care and attention. We were all babies, once – each one of us. A small miracle. For all newborn babies, everywhere, we give you thanks, O Lord.

Alternative assembly topics
- Christmas presents;
- St Nicholas;
- Christmas celebrations in other lands.

Development
- Ask the children to describe six events of the story of Jesus' nativity, using both words and pictures to create their own Christmas story cartoon.
- Ask a volunteer new mother, with the ability and willingness to talk with children, to come into the class and talk about looking after a baby, linking this to health education if appropriate.
- *We remember Jesus' birthday – what other birthdays do lots of people remember or celebrate?* (For example, Shakespeare, the Queen.) Make a calendar of famous people's birthdays.

Links
SEAL: New beginnings; Good to be me.
PSHE: 1a. To recognise their worth as individuals.

Bethlehem

Christian core

Bethlehem, the City of David, is also the place where Jesus was born. It was on the hills around Bethlehem that the angels delivered their message of 'peace on earth, goodwill toward men' (Luke 2: 10–14).

Other key ideas

Bethlehem is an important city for Jews and Christians alike; people of both the Muslim and Christian faiths inhabit the city and many pilgrims visit. Yet nowhere is the need for peace and understanding in the world today better demonstrated than in the troubled town of Bethlehem.

Music for assembling

If you are not averse to introducing an assembly with voices, a carol is the obvious choice at Christmas. For a less obvious choice of carol try the modern classic, *Nativity Carol*, by John Rutter (4' 50"). (*Refer to Index for alternative suggestions.*)

Song on the CD

'Bethlehem stills' is a new carol that tells an old story. Schools with competent junior choirs might attempt to sing the first three bars of the chorus in thirds (two parts). This song also includes a second voice part.

See photocopiable pages 56 and 57.

Alternative music for singing

■ 'Here we go up to Bethlehem', by the late Sydney Carter (*SRTY*, 1), is sung to the traditional tune of 'Here we go round the Mulberry Bush' and is best sung unaccompanied. Children can make up their own verses.

■ Many traditional carols mention Bethlehem: 'O little town of Bethlehem' by Phillips Brooks (*WCV*, 97) proclaims the angels' message of peace (omit some verses).

Resources

Appropriate images from the CD include: 'Bethlehem conflict' and 'Bethlehem dividing wall'.

Presentation

I wonder if there is anybody here who has ever been told to 'Be still!'

Ask for a show of hands. You might then interrogate one or two children, or teachers, about when and why they were asked to 'be still'.

What does 'be still' mean? Sometimes it may simply mean 'stop fidgeting', but it can mean much more than that. An aunt of mine was never still; she was always cooking or cleaning or ironing. She wasn't even still when she was watching TV; she would always be knitting or sewing. She wasn't a fidget; she was just a busy person who was never still.

When we sing the carol about Bethlehem being 'still', we are not talking about a town that has stopped knitting or fidgeting or being busy; we are talking about a place that has an air of calm and peace. That is just how I imagine Bethlehem when Jesus was born in that manger one bright, starlit night over two thousand years ago. A peaceful place.

Jesus grew up preaching a message of peace. Sadly, people still need to be reminded of that message today, especially in Bethlehem.

You may, using your judgement, interject some relevant information about recent trouble in the Middle East. You may want to show 'Bethlehem conflict', or 'Bethlehem dividing wall' from the CD.

Reflection or prayer

Let us be still. While we are still, let us hold in our thoughts all people who do not, at this time, enjoy peace in their lands, especially the people of Bethlehem.

Dear Heavenly Father, at this special time, when we celebrate the joyous birth of the babe in a manger and remember the message of peace that he brought, we pray that the guns

and bombs may be stilled all over the world and that hatred be banished from men's hearts. Amen.

Alternative assembly topics
■ Pilgrimage;
■ The wise men's visit to Bethlehem;
■ Peace campaigners.

Development
■ See how many carols and songs you can find that mention Bethlehem. List all the ways that Bethlehem is described in these songs.
■ Write your own poem about Bethlehem today. Begin each line: 'Bethlehem is…' (You could write a different verse beginning each line: 'Bethlehem was…').
■ Plan an imaginary trip to Bethlehem – a pilgrimage. Work out your flights, itinerary, timings and costs. *Where would you fly from? Which places would you plan to see when you got there?*

Links
SEAL: Getting on and falling out (empathy).
PSHE: 2f. To resolve differences.

The sign of the cross

Christian core

The Easter story is centred on Christ's death on the cross and his triumphant resurrection. The story is remembered and retold each year, just like the story of Christmas. Palm Sunday begins Holy Week; on Good Friday, Christ's death is remembered and on Easter Sunday, his resurrection. The next six weeks, until Ascension Day, are designated Eastertide. Unlike Christmas, Easter is a moveable feast between 21 March and 25 April. The Easter story can be found in Mark 11: 15 and 16 (entry into Jerusalem).

Other key ideas

Signs and symbols are used to represent something beyond the literal (think of road signs) and they are a common feature of religious practice, for example the Hindu *aum* sign. The cross is an ancient symbol. In the form adopted by Christians, it is used to remind them of Christ's sacrifice on the cross and to proclaim their Christianity. The sign of the cross is also used as a blessing.

Music for assembling

Johann Sebastian Bach, *Jesu, Joy of Man's Desiring*, BMV 147, arranged for orchestra (3'12"). *(Refer to Index for alternative suggestions.)*

Song on the CD

'Easter hymn' includes parts for glockenspiels or chime bars to give the tune a triumphant, bell-like quality. The tuned percussion part is not difficult but should be practised.

See photocopiable pages 58 and 59.

Alternative music for singing

■ 'Lift high the cross' by George W. Kitchin and Michael R. Newbolt (*SOP*, 83), to the tune 'Crucifer', is a fine, rousing hymn of praise and you have the option of selecting suitable verses from the 11 available!

■ Traditional Easter hymns tend to be theologically difficult, so you might favour a general hymn of praise, or try 'Every star shall sing a carol' by Sydney Carter, (*SRTY*, 3 – selected verses).

Resources

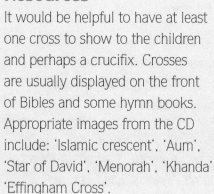

It would be helpful to have at least one cross to show to the children and perhaps a crucifix. Crosses are usually displayed on the front of Bibles and some hymn books. Appropriate images from the CD include: 'Islamic crescent', 'Aum', 'Star of David', 'Menorah', 'Khanda' 'Effingham Cross'.

Presentation

Show and discuss the cross or crucifix.

What is it used for? Why is it here on this book? This cross is called a crucifix because it has an image of Jesus on it.

It is very easy to draw or make a cross; it is a very simple, clear sign so you will find different types of crosses in many places. Can you think of any flags that have crosses on them?

Discuss the Union Jack, St Andrew's cross, St George's cross and so on.

You may want to touch upon other religious symbols, perhaps creating a slideshow from the CD, using images such as: Islam's Crescent moon, Judaism's Star of David and Sikhism's Khanda. Some children may be able to explain the significance of such symbols, which may be important to them.

This cross (show again) is a very special one to Christians. You will see it on churches, in churches, on bibles and even worn as a badge or a piece of jewellery. Display the photograph of the Effingham Cross. Christians in Effingham in America have built a cross that is 198 feet tall with 180 tons of steel. It is as tall as a 20-storey building and is the largest cross in the world.

The cross reminds Christians of the day when Jesus, who had done no wrong, was killed. But because Christians believe that Jesus lives on in our hearts, the cross is a symbol of triumph, joy and hope. Christians do not display the cross because they are sad but because they are happy and it shows that they are Christians. During some church services people make the sign of the cross on their chests.

Demonstrate this – left to right for western Christendom – it is used as a kind of blessing. In this or subsequent assemblies you could tell the Easter narrative in a form appropriate to the children.

Reflection or prayer

At this joyful Eastertide, we remember Jesus' sacrifice on the cross and the triumphant message of love and hope that he brought to the world. Dear Heavenly Father, when we see the sign of the cross, may we remember your love for us and in remembering, show our love for each other. Amen.

Alternative assembly topics
- Palm Sunday;
- Handel's *Messiah*;
- Religious symbols.

Development
- Make diagrams, like flow charts, setting down the main events of Easter in the order in which they happened. Older children might use Bibles as a source for this task – with a little direction.
- Visit a local church and see how many times the cross can be seen there. The cross, known also as the 'rood', used to be mounted high on a 'rood screen' in churches.
- Arrange a visit by a local priest. Ask him or her to talk about the use of the cross in church and on robes, and to explain terms such as 'rood' and 'crucifer'.

Links
SEAL: Getting on and falling out (empathy).
PSHE: 2i. To appreciate the range of national, regional, religious and ethnic identities in the United Kingdom.

Sing a song or Psalm

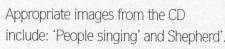

Christian core

In the Old Testament of the Bible, poems and songs written thousands of years ago are collected together in the Book of Psalms. Although written long ago, Christians can still identify with many of the sentiments that they express and 'give thanks unto the Lord … sing psalms unto him' and 'talk of all his wondrous works' (Psalm 105: 1–2).

Other key ideas

On special occasions and especially when we are happy, we sing. People have been singing praises to God since ancient times and singing forms part of religious observance in Christianity and other faiths: the Sikh 'scriptures' in the *Guru Granth Sahib*, for example, are worship hymns.

Music for assembling

Johann Sebastian Bach, *Sheep May Safely Graze*, Cantata No. 208, BMV 208 (4' 57"). (*Refer to Index for alternative suggestions.*)

Song on the CD

'Clap, clap your hands!' is loosely based upon Psalm 47 and is a straightforward hymn of praise. Keep the tune moving and cheerful. This song also includes parts for recorder and untuned percussion on the CD.

See photocopiable pages 60 and 61.

Alternative music for singing

■ There are a number of suitable psalm arrangements in the primary school canon, and this is the perfect opportunity to use one

of them. 'The Lord's my shepherd' is often a favourite (*WCV*, 38).

■ 'Lord of the years' by Timothy Dudley-Smith (*SOP*, 333) is one of those few modern hymns of praise that has become a standard in the writer's lifetime. It fits comfortably within the primary child's singing range.

Resources

Appropriate images from the CD include: 'People singing' and Shepherd'.

Presentation

I am going to tell you a secret. Don't tell anyone, but I sing in the bath. Actually, I not only sing in the bath, I sing in the shower as well. My voice is not really very good, but when I get into the shower in the morning and open my mouth to sing, a wonderful noise comes out. Suddenly I am as good as McFly (change name as appropriate). I am, I really am. I would prove it to you right now but I forgot to bring my bathroom with me.

Does anybody here sing in the bathroom like me? Bathrooms add an echo to your voice, so most people are better singers in the bathroom; that is why many people sing there. Of course, singing is particularly good at making you feel happy. So we sing in the bathroom, we sing along with our favourite recordings, we sing in school and we sing in church. Some people even sing at work.

SCHOLASTIC
www.scholastic.co.uk

Assemble and sing! For ages 7-11

 You could show the 'People singing' image from the CD, at this point.

A long, long time ago, people made up songs and poems when they were working – in those days this may well have taken place out in the fields and on the hills when they were looking after herds of animals. (Show the image of the shepherd with his flock.) We know this because in the Old Testament of the Bible there is a collection of 150 songs and poems known as the Book of Psalms. Most of them are happy songs – songs that celebrate the wonderful world that the writers could see all around them. They are songs of praise to God. One of the psalms tells people to be happy and to praise God in dance, with trumpets, with cymbals and with songs. We don't know what the tunes sounded like, because it is such a long time ago in history, but we can still sing these psalms today, to modern tunes – in the bathroom, if we like.

Illustrate if appropriate: children may sing a psalm or listen to Howard Goodall's setting of Psalm 23, as featured in The Vicar of Dibley.

Reflection or prayer

We give thanks for the gift of music and singing. Help us to celebrate the wonders of the world around us and to sing praises, like the psalmist of ancient times, and 'make a joyful noise unto the Lord'.

Alternative assembly topics
- Celebration of a famous composer;
- Albert Schweitzer;
- St Cecilia's Day.

Development
- Write a poem or song of praise for your town, village or city. Search for appropriate photographs for which a selection of quotations from Psalms (23, 41, 121, 150) could be used as captions. Make a class display of the selection.
- Take a suitable psalm, such as Psalm 100, and make an illustrated version of it using a selected art medium or computer programme.

Links
SEAL: Good to be me (empathy).
PSHE: 2e. To reflect on spiritual issues;
2i. To appreciate the range of national, regional, religious and ethnic identities in the United Kingdom; 4b. To think about the lives of people living in other places and times, and people with different values and customs.

A number of things

Christian core

God's world is full of mystery. Christians are all filled with awe by this amazing and yet still mysterious world, and are moved to celebrate and give thanks for all of God's wonderful creation: 'In the beginning, God created the heaven and the Earth' (Genesis 1: 1).

Other key ideas

The world is an amazing place and is full of an astonishing variety of creatures. We know much about how and where many of these creatures live, but we still do not know everything. The variety of creation fills us with awe and wonder and we cannot explain it all. There are many different stories and myths used to tap into this mystery and to celebrate the creation of the world.

Music for assembling

Camille Saint-Saëns, *Carnival of the Animals*. Both 'The Aquarium' (2' 31") and 'The Swan' (2' 47") are soothing. Alternatively, children could march in to 'The Royal March of the Lion' (2' 16"). (*Refer to Index for alternative suggestions.*)

Song on the CD

'Creation song' starts off with a verse about an aardvark and a zho (Tibetan cow); the song could be 26 verses long! It is meant to be fun, so sing brightly but not too fast – allow the words to be heard. Try embellishing with percussion and other sound effects.

See photocopiable pages 62 and 63.

Alternative music for singing

■ 'All things bright and beautiful' by Cecil F. Alexander will fit the bill here (*WCV*, 75 – choice of two tunes; *C&P*, 3 offers yet another tune). The musically adventurous might even try John Rutter's rhythmic arrangement.

■ 'All creatures of our God and King' (after St Francis of Assisi, *WCV*, 8), to Ralph Vaughan Williams' rousing tune, can readily become a primary school favourite.

Resources

Appropriate images from the CD include: 'Butterfly', 'Elephant', 'Otter' 'Porcupine', 'Robin' and 'Terrapin'.

Presentation

'The world is full of a number of things, I'm sure we should all be as happy as kings', wrote the storyteller and poet Robert Louis Stevenson. He was right. In particular, the world is full of an amazing variety of living creatures, from the smallest bug to the largest whale. Some living things are so small that they can only be seen using a microscope. We know there are about 10,000 different types (species) of creatures called protisans and they are made of just one single living cell – things don't come much smaller than that. Then there are at least 30,000 different types of fish, nearly 5,000 species of mammal, 10,000 species of bird and at least one million species of insect – up to

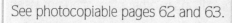

10,000 new insects are being discovered each year. What an amazing place the world is!

Two of the creatures I find most interesting are the kangaroo and the elephant: the kangaroo because it keeps its babies in its pocket – a really useful trick – and the elephant, because it appears to have a tail at both ends. You can't always tell whether it is coming or going. What creatures do you find most interesting?

Include some interaction with the children. Ask them to explain why they find a particular creature interesting. You can talk about some of the creatures in the worship song – the spider monkey; the sloth; the zho – or prepare a slideshow of amazing creatures using images from the CD.

Reflection or prayer

Dear Heavenly Father, we thank you for the world and all the amazing creatures in it; for the tiny shrew in the long grass, for the sleek shark in the ocean deep, for the soaring skylark hovering above the meadow. For all of your creation, we thank you. Amen.

We share the world with a multitude of creatures; all are part of God's creation. Help us to remember that

there is room enough for us all in this world and that the world would be a poorer place without its amazing population of mammals, fish, insects and birds. For all these things, O God, we give thanks. Amen.

Alternative assembly topics
- Conservation of wildlife;
- Caring for animals;
- Pets;
- RSPCA;
- Creation stories.

Development
- Examine the pattern of the verses of 'Creation Song' and commission groups of pupils to write verses for other letters of the alphabet, in the same style.
- Get each pupil to write a short, illustrated biography of one of the 'multitude of creatures'.
- Older pupils might study the creation story in Genesis. Compare this with other creation stories. *Is there a sense in which any of them can be 'true'?*

Links
SEAL: New beginnings.
PSHE: 2i. To appreciate the range of national, regional, religious and ethnic identities in the United Kingdom.

Raise a laugh

Christian core

Christians thank God for the world and all his gifts; humour is surely one of these. Christians are not afraid of laughter and relish the opportunity, with the psalmist, to 'make a joyful noise unto the Lord' (Psalm 100). 'The kingdom of God… is joy' (Romans 14: 17).

Other key ideas

Laughter is one of the joys of life, a gift to be shared and cherished.

Music for assembling

Claude Debussy, 'Golliwog's Cakewalk' (2'53") from *The Children's Corner* – an upbeat, buoyant piece of music. (*Refer to Index for alternative suggestions.*)

Song on the CD

'Drink the laughing waters of life' is open to a free interpretation, but the rhythmic pattern of the piece should be stressed. Avoid over-doing the onomatopoeic chuckle in the chorus.

See photocopiable pages 64 and 65.

Alternative music for singing

■ 'Give me oil in my lamp', traditional (*C&P*, 43), needs to be performed cheerfully, if not with tambourines and streamers!

■ For true optimism and cheer, try 'I'll go in the strength of the Lord' by Ivor Bosanko and Edward Turney (*SOP*, 329).

Resources

A Christmas cracker. Appropriate images from the CD include: 'Clowns' and 'Ladies laughing'.

Presentation

> Now, here's a cracker. What time is it when an elephant sits on your fence? Time to get a new fence. Oh, you've heard that one. Here's another cracker.

At this point it would be appropriate to produce a cracker if you have one left over from Christmas. Get a child to pull it with you.

Show the 'Clowns' image from the CD, or tell a selection of jokes in succession:

> What do you call a monkey that has swallowed a bomb? *Babooom!*
>
> Why do ducks have yellow feet? *So that you can't see them when they are swimming upside down in custard!*
>
> What goes left, right, left, right, left, right (talk very fast) left, right, left, right, left, right, left, right – CLUNK? *A centipede with a wooden leg.*

SCHOLASTIC
www.scholastic.co.uk

◀ Continue in this vein for a while with pupil interaction if you can manage it, while keeping an eye out for any inappropriate jokes.

It's not often that we tell jokes in assembly but I have done it today for a reason. We often celebrate in assembly when one of you has done some good work, or won an award, or a sporting contest – but being able to make people laugh and feel happy is just as much a gift of God as having a sharp brain or excellent coordination. So today we celebrate the gift of laughter.

Show 'Laughing ladies' image from the CD at this point as a demonstration of the positive effects of laughing.

In my primary school we had a very good teacher called Mr Spratt. He was an excellent pianist and we all liked him very much, but we were a bit frightened of him. No one, but no one, misbehaved in Mr Spratt's class. One day, he was teaching singing to the whole school. He told us to stand up straight and open our lungs and SING. (He was a bit cross.) He went over to the piano, and sat down. The stool collapsed completely and Mr Spratt ended up on his back with his legs in the air. We howled with laughter – and so did Mr Spratt, until the tears ran down his face. I was never frightened of him again (although I still didn't dare misbehave in his class!).

Reflection or prayer

Dear Heavenly Father, we thank you for the gift of laughter and for the joy we experience when we make each other laugh. Help us to use this gift to make the world a better place. Amen.

Dear God, we know that life can be very hard sometimes. May we live with your love and joy in our hearts so that we spread happiness wherever we go and bring joy into the lives of others. Amen.

Alternative assembly topics
- Making a happy school;
- Comic Relief;
- Jokes that hurt;
- Bullying.

Development
- Have a 'share a joke' board where children post funny stories (carefully written and approved).
- Imagine: a teacher comes to school looking miserable (perish the thought!). Working in small groups, devise three ways to cheer him or her up.
- Working in pairs devise ten rules for a happy home (or classroom).

Links
SEAL: Getting on and falling out; Say no to bullying (social skills).
PSHE: 3a. To know what makes a healthy lifestyle; **4a.** To realise that their actions affect themselves and others.

Good morning

Christian core

It is a Christian duty to love one's neighbour, but in the Sermon on the Mount, Jesus also taught that you should love your enemies: 'If ye salute your brethren only, what do ye more than others?' (Matthew 5: 43–48).

Other key ideas

The world is a beautiful place that is made even more so by friendship and love of one another, an idea promoted by many religions: in Judaism, for example, the Torah states, 'Love your neighbour like yourself' (Leviticus (Old Testament) 19: 18).

Music for assembling

Edward Elgar, *Chanson de Matin*, Op. 15 No. 2 (3'02"). (*Refer to Index for alternative suggestions.*)

Song on the CD

The song 'Good morning' not only celebrates the new day dawning, but is also in praise of friendship. This song also includes parts for recorder and tuned percussion on the CD.

See photocopiable pages 66 and 67.

Alternative music for singing

You might use the familiar 'Morning has broken' by Eleanor Farjeon (*C&P*, 1) or perhaps the short but apposite morning hymn 'Father we thank thee for the night' by Rebecca Weston (*WCV*, 4).

Resources

Appropriate images on the CD include: 'Sunrise' and 'Greetings'. You may want show the 'Sunrise' photograph when introducing the song or as the children are assembling.

Presentation

Good morning!

I have already said that greeting many times this morning; have you? It is very rare that we don't say some friendly words of greeting when we first meet someone. If we didn't do so, the world would become a very strange and unfriendly place indeed.

Imagine if I went to the doctor, and instead of being greeted by 'Good morning', the doctor began by saying 'What do you want?'

You can give other similar examples.

We do, of course, use other phrases that serve the same purpose. Can you think of any?

You could spend a few minutes exploring the kinds of greetings used by adults and children, including slang phrases.

Show 'Greetings' from the CD, which shows a child and grandparent greeting each other with a hug.

When we wish someone a 'good morning', we are not only wishing him or her a pleasant day, we are also opening the door to friendship. If I said to new parents visiting the school for the first time 'Who are you?', it wouldn't be a very good beginning. I am sure I would ask them who they were at some point, but it would not be the first thing that I would say. Being friendly is the best start to a good morning and a good day. As we have just been singing, the world is a beautiful place, but it is made even more beautiful by friendship.

And now we are going to finish by being both friendly and grown-up. Let's make this a particularly good start to the day. I want you to shake hands with and say good morning to the people on either side of you.

Reflection or prayer

Dear Heavenly Father, we don't know what will happen today – what problems or pleasures await us – but we will try our best to make today a good day for those around us. Help us to take pleasure in your beautiful world and to do what we can to make it an even better place. Amen.

Let us give thanks for the world and all its wonders – for the green grass of the fields, for the clouds in the sky above us, and for the friends who stand beside us. Lord, hear our prayer.

Alternative assembly topics
- Making friends;
- Caring for the environment;
- Miracles.

Development
- Make a list of all the ways in which different people greet each other (you might touch upon other languages and cultures too).
- Design a 'welcome' board for the entrance to the school. *What might you include on it? How do we show that we wish to be friends with someone?*
- Paint, or describe in some other way, a memorable daybreak.

Links
SEAL: New beginnings; Relationships (social skills).
PSHE: 1a. To face new challenges positively; **2f.** To resolve differences.

In the small things

Christian core

Christians see the hand of God in the wonders of his creation, in the small things as well as the large. Christians are expected to show the love of God through the way in which they live their lives: 'Let your light so shine before men that they may see your good works' (Matthew 5: 16).

Other key ideas

If we look closely at the world, we discover that, even in the smallest things, there is beauty. Our own beauty (or goodness) is also shown in the small things, in the small acts of kindness that we do in our daily lives.

Music for assembling

Piotr Ilyich Tchaikovsky, *The Nutcracker Suite*, Op. 71a, 'Miniature Overture' (3' 13"). (*Refer to Index for alternative suggestions.*)

Song on the CD

'In the small things' is a song of wonder and awe. Although not musically difficult, it requires competent reading and precise diction if the words are to be heard and to be correctly married to the tune. Note the alternative major chord ending to the final verse – known as a *Tierce de Picardie*. This song also includes parts for chime bars or glockenspiel on the CD.

See photocopiable pages 68 and 69.

Alternative music for singing

■ Folliot Pierpoint's 'For the beauty of the 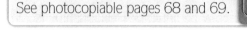 Earth' (*WCV*, 23 or *C&P*, 11) is well suited.

■ Alternatively, you could use any decent hymn of praise, such as the traditional 'Now thank we all our God', to the tune 'Gracias', by Geoffrey Beaumont (*C&P*, 38)

Resources

Appropriate images on the CD include: 'Baby's hand', 'Butterfly', 'Ocean' and 'Robin'.

Presentation

Now here's an interesting thought – I was small and beautiful once and so were you! Some people (perhaps your mum, dad, grandma and grandad) probably think that you still are. Yes, I was small and beautiful when I was born, or so my mother told me. Now, of course, I am not so small.

It is surprising how beautiful small things can be; if you look closely at a butterfly or at a flower, especially under a microscope, a whole world of beauty is revealed. Even a snowflake reveals itself to be a thing of beauty when it is examined closely. Can you think of any other examples?

■SCHOLASTIC
www.scholastic.co.uk

Assemble and sing! For ages 7-1

Discuss ideas with the children.

If you have ever watched nature programmes on the TV, you will have seen things of amazing beauty in even the smallest of creatures, living both in the sea and on the land. Many people believe that there is nothing more beautiful than the natural world around us and that there is heavenly beauty right here on Earth, if only we open our eyes to see it.

Perhaps show and discuss one or two images from the CD at this point.

There is goodness (and that is a thing of beauty) in all of us – no matter how big we are – and it shows itself in what we do. Simple acts of kindness – offering a helping hand when it is needed, befriending the friendless or lonely – these are the things that show the beauty within us. It's all in the small things.

Reflection or prayer

Dear Heavenly Father, your universe is vast and we are very small, but in both there is beauty. Help us to show the beauty that is within us by how we treat each other.

Dear God, we give you thanks for the small things. Mighty mountains and vast oceans are wonderful but so too are tiny wrens singing in the hedgerow, and delicate flowers

 growing in the meadow. For all this beauty, we give you thanks. Amen.

Alternative assembly topics
- Conservation;
- Celebration of a great scientist, musician or doctor.

Development
- Use microscopes and hand lenses to examine objects closely. Encourage children to describe precisely what they see.
- Using digital cameras, ask children to take close-up photos of natural objects occurring in the local environment close to the school. Enlarge and print the best examples.
- Working in groups, let children devise a list of a few small ways in which their town or village could be improved.

Links
SEAL: New beginnings (social skills).
PSHE: 4a. To care about other people's feelings; **5a.** To care for the environment.

The light of the world

Christian core

There is an enduring image, based on the text in St John's Gospel (8: 12), of Jesus represented as 'the Light of the World', often reinforced in people's minds by the pre-Raphaelite painting by William Holman Hunt. Jesus is seen by Christians as, in the words of the Nunc Dimittis, 'a light to lighten the Gentiles, and the glory of thy people Israel' (Luke 2: 32).

Other key ideas

Light is a frequently used religious symbol, a potent image for hope and love: Hindus celebrate the festival of lights (Diwali) in late October; in December, in Scandinavia, the Sancta Lucia Festival celebrating light and growth takes place.

Music for assembling

Wolfgang Amadeus Mozart, Sonata for two pianos in D major, K448, 'Andante' (3' 10"). (*Refer to Index for alternative suggestions.*)

Song on the CD

'Shine!' must be sung cheerfully and at a decent pace. The last verse key change can be omitted if there are insufficient older voices to cope with the step up. This song also includes a part for untuned percussion on the CD.

See photocopiable pages 70 and 71.

Alternative music for singing

■ 'Light up the fire' by Sue McClellan, John Pac and Keith Ryecroft (*C&P*, 55) and 'Give me oil in my lamp', traditional (*C&P*, 43), are both suitable contemporary songs.

■ 'When a knight won his spurs' by Jan Struther (*WCV*, 66) is a more traditional alternative.

Resources

The hall should be dimly lit beforehand; large candle(s) and a taper; matches or a lighter; appropriate images from the CD include: *'The Light of the World'* and 'Diwali'.

Presentation

It is not very light in here. I am going to do what people used to do when it was dark, before electric lights were invented. I am going to light a fire – don't be frightened; it is only a very small fire.

Light a large candle. You might also allow a child from each class to light a candle, using a taper, under close adult supervision. Take time over this, as it will add to the atmosphere.

Light is a wonderful thing, especially the light generated by a flame.
A flame seems to be a living creature; it moves, and changes as it moves.
I love watching flames burn in an open fire; you can see all sorts of shapes in them. I like to try to see faces and creatures in the flames. People used to burn candles for light, but the flames also brought something warm and comforting into their homes.

It is not surprising that Christians think of Jesus arriving in the world in the same way as we think of light arriving in a room when a candle is lit. Jesus had a message of love that brought hope to everyone – so it was as if someone had lit a giant candle and people could see clearly at last. Following the teaching of Jesus brings light into people's lives and, like the light of a candle, this is something warm and comforting.

You might now read the words from St John's Gospel given below (John 8: 12):

'Then spake Jesus again unto them, saying, I am the light of the world: he that followeth me shall not walk in darkness, but shall have the light of life'.

You could spend a few minutes at this point talking about the Holman Hunt painting (image from the CD). Note particularly: Jesus is dressed as a king, he is holding a lantern, he is knocking on the door, the door does not have a handle on the outside and dawn is about to break. Alternatively, show the Diwali photograph and discuss how candles are used as part of this celebration.

Reflection or prayer

Jesus came to bring light into the world. Help us to bring light into the lives of the people that we meet. Amen.

Dear Heavenly Father, there are many people who have little light in their lives – the hungry, the oppressed, the poor, the sick, the lonely – we pray for them and for those whose lives are dedicated to helping them. May their lives shine with the light of your love. Amen.

Alternative assembly topics

- St Lucia;
- The lives of people who brought light into the lives of the suffering or oppressed; for example, Martin Luther King, Mother Teresa, Elizabeth Fry or Leonard Cheshire;
- Diwali.

Development

- Look closely at the words of the hymn 'Shine'. Talk about the rhythm and the pattern of the words. Encourage children to write a verse of their own.
- Light makes an excellent subject for a painting lesson: look at how various famous painters have interpreted light in their paintings (Turner, for example). Choose a suitable subject for a painting exercise, such as light falling on one side of a still life arrangement or sunset behind a townscape.

Links

SEAL: Relationships (social skills).
PSHE: 2e. To reflect on spiritual issues;
2i. To appreciate the range of national, regional, religious and ethnic identities in the United Kingdom.

A good name

Christian core

The Bible teaches that we shall be known by what we do; not who we are but what we are (Matthew 7: 20). Therefore we should all strive to be good people: 'A good name is rather to be chosen than great riches' (Proverbs 22: 1).

Other key ideas

Whichever name we are given by our parents, a good name, in the sense of a worthy and desirable reputation, is something that has to be earned.

Music for assembling

Franz Schubert, Symphony No. 3 in D (D. 200), second movement, 'Allegretto' (4' 39"). (*Refer to Index for alternative suggestions.*)

Song on the CD

'A good name' demands clear diction, but the names should not prove too difficult for children to pronounce. This song also includes a part for recorder or tuned percussion.

See photocopiable pages 72 and 73.

Alternative music for singing

■ 'Heavenly Father, may thy blessing' by William Charter Piggott (*WCV*, 61 and *C&P*, 62) contains a fine catalogue of virtues.
■ 'At the name of Jesus' by Caroline Noel (*C&P*, 58 and *SOP*, 118) can be sung to two fine tunes, of which children tend to prefer Camberwell. The more satisfactory accompaniment is given in *SOP*.

Resources

Wear a jumper and a jacket. An appropriate image from the CD is: 'Dennis the Menace'.

Presentation

I am getting a bit forgetful. Yesterday I forgot to put the bin out for the dustman; I also forgot where I put my mobile phone and the number on my car number plate. None of this is very serious – except for one other lapse of memory. I am not sure who I am. Do you know?

Allow as much interaction here as possible.

Well, that is all very interesting, but I think I had better check. Let's see whose clothes I'm wearing.

Take off the jumper and read the name label:

It says 'Austin Reed'. I don't think that's my name.

Read jacket label: Ralph Lauren? Search through your wallet and read out name on credit cards or driving licence:

That seems to settle it. My name is _____. Ah yes, I remember now! Let's see if I can remember your names.

You can start at one end of a row and recite the names. Use the youngest children, as their names will be least familiar. Alternatively, let the children recite their own names.

These all seem very good names to me.

I once knew a boy called Wayne (choose the name very carefully!). He seemed to have a perfectly good name, but actually he had a bad name – a very bad name. You would walk past his house and you would hear his mother scream, 'Wayne!!! COME HERE!' If something went wrong in school, and you asked 'Who did this?', the answer nearly always came back, 'It was Wayne'. It wasn't always Wayne and sometimes he was accused unfairly, but unfortunately he had got himself a bad reputation. He had got himself a bad name.

You could discuss fictional characters who have a bad name such as Dennis the Menace (see image from the CD) or Bart Simpson.

Everyone likes to be known, but we all like to be known for good reasons. If you have a good name, people will trust you, they will respect you, they will admire you and they will want to be friends with you – they may even try to be like you. You don't have to do amazing things to get a good name. You don't have to be especially clever or brave or good looking. But to earn a good name, you do have to be the sort of person whom people like to be with: someone who is caring and honest; someone who is a good friend.

Reflection or prayer

Help us to be honest and kind and to care about each other. When our names are spoken, may they be spoken in a good way, for a 'good name is to be preferred above riches'.

The name of Jesus is holy and Jesus is forever remembered as a man of great goodness. Help us to follow his footsteps in the path of love and truth. In the name of Jesus Christ, Amen.

Alternative assembly topics
■ People with good and bad names: Mother Teresa, Hitler;
■ Christenings.

Development
■ Get children to write down two good attributes of the person sitting next to them and discuss as a class. The idea is for everyone to feel positive about him or herself.
■ Talk about people who have a good reputation and discuss why this is so.
■ Research the most popular names today.
■ Children might like to change lines of the song to include their own names.

Links
SEAL: Say no to bullying; Getting on and falling out; Good to be me.
PSHE: 1b. To recognise their worth as individuals; **4a.** To know that their actions affect themselves and others; **4e.** To recognise and challenge stereotypes.

Who cares?

Christian core

By his example and his teaching, Christ taught that we should 'love one another'. It therefore matters how we live and it matters to Christians how other people live too. In particular, Christians should care about people in need, as Jesus illustrated in the parable of the Good Samaritan. The definitive statement is contained in the Sermon on the Mount (Matthew 5: 1–12).

Other key ideas

Caring is important. We need to care about ourselves as well as about each other. Charitable acts are a worthy human endeavour: giving to the poor and needy is one of the five pillars of the Islamic faith (Zakat).

Music for assembling

Joseph Haydn, Trumpet Concerto in E flat major, 'Andante' (3' 47"). (*Refer to Index for alternative suggestions.*)

Song on the CD

'God cares' needs a little practice to ensure that children do not sing through the rests, as the silence between notes is as vital as the notes themselves.

See photocopiable pages 74 and 75.

Alternative music for singing

■ 'When I needed a neighbour' by Sydney Carter (*C&P*, 65 – a very simple arrangement). Keep it moving to avoid it becoming a dirge.
■ The struggle to follow Christ's example

forms the core of 'He who would valiant be' by Percy Dearmer and John Bunyan (*WCV*, 40 and *C&P*, 44 in a lower key) is a good sing, although the language is a little difficult.

Resources

An appropriate images from the CD is: 'The Red Cross'.

Presentation

Two of the saddest words I can think of are 'don't care'. Whenever I hear those two words uttered, I usually find it quite upsetting. You see, the people who 'don't care' do not care about other people – they don't care what happens to them. They are selfish, mean-minded and cruel, and in the end, rather sad creatures because other people eventually cease to care about them and soon they don't even care about themselves.

Jesus taught that we should care about each other, and it is right that we should. Just imagine a world where nobody cared about anybody. It would be a totally selfish world, but it would also be a completely mad world.

Imagine, you get on a bus and buy a ticket to the station, but the bus driver goes to the zoo. You complain: 'I bought a ticket to the station and you've gone somewhere else!' 'Don't care', says the bus driver. You show your work to your teacher. 'Look, I have got all my sums right!' 'Don't care', says your teacher. 'Mum, you have put a bag of nuts in my lunch box and nuts make me ill!' 'Don't care', says mum.

Interject a few of your own examples to demonstrate that a world without caring people just would not work.

Luckily for all of us, most people do care. The teachers and I care if children in this school are unhappy. I care that this school is a safe and interesting place. I even care when the football team loses. Caring about other people is important. Caring is what will make the world a better place. Some people and organisations are dedicated to caring about other people.

You may want to lengthen the assembly here, by talking about one of the caring organisations and describing the work that they do: for example, Age Concern, the Salvation Army or Macmillan Nurses. Use 'The Red Cross' image from the CD as a visual aid.

Reflection or prayer

Dear Heavenly Father, who showed through the life of Jesus Christ that you care about all of us, help us too to care. Fill us with your love and give us the courage to care, even when we find it difficult to do so.

We pray for all those people who dedicate their lives to helping other people, in organisations such as Christian Aid, the Red Cross and the Salvation Army. Strengthen them in what they do and may their lives shine as an example to us all. Amen.

Alternative assembly topics
■ Organisations that care: Help the Aged, the Samaritans and so on.

Development
■ Research the work of caring organisations. Make a large wall display of the results.
■ Have a debate to choose an organisation for a support campaign. *How do you decide?*
■ Write a fantasy story about 'The mouse who didn't care' (or similar). Older juniors might read these stories to children in the lower classes.

Links
SEAL: Getting on and falling out.
PSHE: 2h. To recognise the role of voluntary groups; **4a.** To know that their actions affect themselves and others and to care about other people's feelings.

Worship of God

Christian core

The worship of God is, of course, part of Christian teaching. The Old Testament exhorts people to 'worship the Lord in the beauty of holiness' (Psalm 96: 9 and Psalm 29: 2).

Other key ideas

People worship God in different places and in different ways, but their purpose in their prayers and worship is often the same.

Music for assembling

Aram Khachaturian, *Spartacus*, 'Adagio of Spartacus and Phrygia' (first three minutes only). (*Refer to Index for alternative suggestions.*)

Song on the CD

'Lord of dome and Lord of spire' focuses on the fact that people follow many different paths in seeking truth. Ideally, one breath should cover the last line, but you should try not to chop up the last three syllables of the line with the taking of breaths.

See photocopiable pages 76 and 77.

Alternative music for singing

'In Christ there is no East or West' by William Dunkerley (*C&P*, 66 or *WCV*, 47 with richer textured accompaniment plus an alternative tune) has very apposite words.

Resources

Appropriate images from the CD include: 'Church', 'Cathedral', 'Mosque' and 'Synagogue'.

Presentation

This is a true story, which you may want to tell the children, or adapt.

Many years ago, an uncle of mine cut a lawn with scissors – nail scissors. He was in the army at the time and as a punishment he had been told to cut a thousand blades of grass from the lawn in front of the guardhouse. When he had finished, the duty sergeant sat down and counted every single blade; then the sergeant made my uncle start all over again because he was one blade short (or so he said).

There are many less painful ways of cutting a lawn – let's see how many we can think of.

Encourage the children to contribute (electric mowers, scythes, petrol mowers and so on).

Now these machines may be different but they all have one thing in common: the purpose for which they were designed – cutting the grass.

There is one way in which churches are like lawn mowers (no, you can't cut the lawn with one). Places of worship, like lawn mowers, share a common purpose.

Discuss the children's views here.

Churches are there to provide a place where people can meet and share in the worship of God. How many different places of worship can you think of?

The children can again contribute. Discuss different types of buildings – similar buildings with different names and buildings for different faiths. You might wish to show images of different places of worship from the CD.

All these differences are interesting and sometimes wonderful, but the most important thing about the buildings is not what is different but what is the same: their common purpose, the worship of God.

Reflection or prayer

Lord God, it doesn't matter under what sort of roof we pray – under spire or dome or the sky above – we pray that you will hear our prayers and direct our lives in the ways of honesty and truth. Amen.

We pray that all people, of whatever colour, race or religion, may learn to share the world in peace and harmony as we all share one God.

Alternative assembly topics
- The practices of a particular faith;
- A religious festival;
- The gift of music;
- The differences and similarities between religions.

Development
- Discuss the spires and domes in your area. You could compile a guide to them, including a map or photographs taken with a digital camera.
- Choose a building with a dome or spire and describe what goes on there. *Who uses it? What do they do in the building?*
- You may have the chance to visit a mosque and a church. *Are there any rules that visitors to these places should observe?*

Links
SEAL: Getting on and falling out (social skills).

PSHE: 2f. To resolve differences; **2i.** To appreciate the range of national, regional, religious and ethnic identities in the United Kingdom; **4e.** To recognise and challenge stereotypes.

Just different

Christian core

Christians believe that we are all equal in the sight of God: 'There is neither Greek nor Jew … Barbarian, Scythian, bond nor free: but Christ is all, and in all' (Colossians 3: 11). Moreover, it is impossible for Christians to love God and yet hate the people around them (Luke 10: 27). 'He who loveth God loveth his brother also' (John 4: 20–21).

Other key ideas

We are all different. We differ in appearance, size, age and colour; we also have different skills and interests. Yet none of these things make us better people than our neighbours. As people we are all to be valued equally – not better, not worse – just different.

Music for assembling

Antonin Dvořák, Symphony No. 9 in E minor, Op. 95 (from the *New World*), 'Largo' *(2' 35")*. (*Refer to Index for alternative suggestions.*)

Song on the CD

'Love your neighbour': although a key commandment, the words rarely appear in hymns. This is best sung smoothly. This song includes a part for recorder.

See photocopiable pages 78 and 79.

Alternative music for singing

■ 'He's got the whole world in his hand', traditional (*C&P*, 19; *SOP*, 294).
■ 'We ask that we live' by Donald Swann (*C&P*, 146); the words could not be more appropriate with their entreaty for 'one people and one world'.

Resources

Appropriate images from the CD include: 'Crow', 'Rabbit', 'Camels' and 'Monkeys'.

Presentation

Now, here is an interesting fact. I read the other day that crows are very good at arithmetic. It's true! Apparently they have been tested by scientists and, under special conditions, it has been proved that they can count all the way up to two. That's very clever. Perhaps they could do my job when I have to teach you arithmetic. No, that is a very silly idea.

When discussing the different animals below, show pictures of some of them using the slideshow feature on the CD.

So, crows are better at arithmetic than say, rabbits – but can they dig a hole in the ground as quickly? Rabbits, of course, are much better at doing that but they are not very good at sitting on the tops of trees and going 'Caw'. On the other hand, whales are very clever animals but they can't go 'Caw' like crows, but then crows can't swim in the ocean. Camels are amazingly clever animals because they can go without a drink for ages, but can they climb trees like monkeys? No, they can't. I find all this terribly confusing; perhaps you can help! Tell me, which animal is best?

Encourage as much interaction as you wish at this point. You may have to underline the distinction between 'favourite' and 'best'. Focus on what particular animals are good at. If a child says a giraffe is the best animal, ask why they think this. Draw out the conclusion that animals are only better at different things, but they are all good animals – not better, not worse, just different.

Human beings are different in all sorts of ways. But they are all human beings, of equal value in God's eyes. We cannot tell how good a book is just by looking at it, or how good a car is by the colour of its paintwork. And so we must learn not to judge people just by their appearance: we are all different – not necessarily better, or worse, just different.

Reflection or prayer

Dear Heavenly Father, we believe that you love us whatever we look like, whatever skills we have, whether we are rich or poor, strong or weak, and whatever our colour, race or nationality. Help us to follow your example and learn to care about all people.

We give thanks to God for all those things that make us different. Help us to celebrate and enjoy these differences, remembering always that we are all equal in your eyes.

Alternative assembly topics

■ People who show or encourage tolerance: Mahatma Gandhi; the Good Samaritan;
■ Love in action: blood donors, for example.

Development

■ Children write down two good ways in which their neighbour in the classroom is different from them (nothing negative, such as ugly, but perhaps related to skills – good at cartwheels, for example). The idea could be expanded into an interesting display.
■ Explore the animal kingdom. *Which animals are the fastest, longest, tallest, heaviest?* and so on. Collect pictures and display the results.
■ Older juniors may look at examples of where people are not treated as 'equal' at home and abroad. *Are there any ways in which we can improve how we treat each other in school?*

Links

SEAL: Relationships; Say no to bullying.
PSHE: 1c. To face new challenges positively; **4a.** To try to see things from other points of view; **2f.** To resolve differences; **2b.** To understand how and why rules and laws are made.

SCHOLASTIC
www.scholastic.co.uk

I don't believe it!

Christian core

The power and importance of hope and love are well attested in the Bible, where they are expressed succinctly by St Paul in 1 Corinthians 13. For Christians, the life and example of Jesus Christ embodies these. 'And now abideth faith, hope and love, these three, but the greatest of these is love.'

Other key ideas

Human feelings such as hope, trust and love are more wonderful and important than devices and possessions. The importance of leading a good life is common to most religions – to Hindus, Buddhists, Muslims and Christians alike.

Music for assembling

Henry Purcell, *Abdelazer*, 'Rondo' (1' 34"). (*Refer to Index for alternative suggestions.*)

Song on the CD

'No greater thing' needs to be sung brightly, with the introduction used as a link between the verses.

See photocopiable pages 80 and 81.

Alternative music for singing

■ Any hymn of praise may be substituted. Michael Saward's 'Christ triumphant', to the tune Guiting Power (*SOP*, 119), is a rousing modern classic – difficult verses can be omitted.

■ 'All the nations of the Earth' by Michael Cockett (*C&P*, 14) bounces along happily... if you will let it. Keep it moving.

Resources

Arrange to have in your pockets or in a bag some 'amazing' things, the properties of which you can discuss with the children. You may want to bring something larger and more dramatic to the assembly – I once rode into the hall on a tandem. The choice is yours. Appropriate images from the CD include: 'Intercity train' and 'Paramedics'.

Presentation

Show an object from your pocket or bag, such as a mobile phone – or use the 'Intercity train' image from the CD and discuss it with the children:

> What do you think of this? It's a little miracle really. You are used to seeing and using these things, but I remember my grandad's words when he was first shown one. 'How does it do that? I don't believe it!'

Show another object – an electric toothbrush, digital camera or similar:

> And what about this? How it works is almost like magic. I know what my grandad would say if he saw one: 'I don't believe it!'

Show a credit card:

> My grandad never used one of these. What is it? What does it do? We did explain to grandad how you could buy things with it, get money from a 'hole

in the wall' and how it knew who you were and how much money you had in the bank. He still didn't like it. 'It's very safe to use', we explained. You can guess what he said: 'I don't believe it!'

The world really is full of amazing things, but human behaviour can be even more amazing. Ordinary human beings can, by astonishing acts of love and devotion, show how much they care about each other. This is much more important than clever machines or devices.

You can expand the assembly here by perhaps adding a story of human devotion, an ordinary routine act of caring, or the work of someone like Mother Teresa or the paramedics (see 'Paramedics' image from the CD).

People care, not because they have to, but because they want to and because it is good to care. Sadly, there are actually some sad people in the world who do not 'care' and I know what my grandad would have said about that. 'I don't believe it!'

Reflection or prayer

It takes courage to care. May we have that courage – the courage to trust, the courage to hope, the courage to care and the courage to love one another.

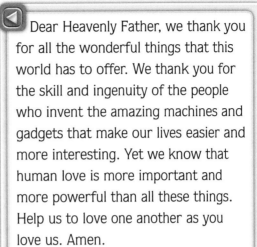

Dear Heavenly Father, we thank you for all the wonderful things that this world has to offer. We thank you for the skill and ingenuity of the people who invent the amazing machines and gadgets that make our lives easier and more interesting. Yet we know that human love is more important and more powerful than all these things. Help us to love one another as you love us. Amen.

Alternative assembly topics
- Caring professions (doctors, teachers and so on);
- The Easter story;
- Charity.

Development
Exploring the issues: make a list of modern inventions, describe how they might improve our lives and how they might make them worse if ill-used. *How do we show that we care about ourselves? How do we show that we care about each other?* Love appears in many songs: 'All You Need is Love'; 'Love Changes Everything'; 'Love is a Many Splendid Thing'; 'The Power of Love'; 'A million Love Songs'. Discuss why love is important.

Links
SEAL: Going for goals (motivation).
PSHE: **1b**. To recognise their worth as individuals; **2f**. Making decisions and explaining choices; **4a**. To know that their actions affect themselves and others.

It's in the book

Christian core

The Old Testament plots the social, moral and religious development of the Jews. Christianity, through the teaching of Christ, moves on from Old Testament teaching. St Paul wrote that 'Christ is the end of the law' (Romans 10: 4) and that loving one's neighbour as one's self is the summation of the law (Galatians 5: 14). Christianity is based upon love, not written laws, and Christians believe that all rules have to be measured against the essential teachings of Jesus – the love of God and of one's neighbour.

Other key ideas

Holy books, such as the Bible for Christians, are special. Other faiths have holy books too, such as the Koran, Torah, Vedas, Upanishads and the Guru Granth Sahib.

Music for assembling

Edvard Grieg, *Holberg Suite*, 'Praeludium' (2' 32"). (*Refer to Index for alternative suggestions.*)

Song on the CD

'Old Testament tales' should be sung cheerily. Use soloists to add variety. You may wish to ensure that the children know the stories to which the verses relate or omit some verses.

See photocopiable pages 82 and 83.

Alternative music for singing

■ Gustav Holst's arrangement fits Percy Dearmer's hymn of praise, 'God is love' (*WCV*, 19) perfectly, although children do tend to bellow parts of the chorus.

■ 'When God made the garden of creation' by Paul Booth (*C&P*, 16) can be shortened by omitting verses, but not the third.

Resources

Have a small selection of books to hand, preferably of differing purposes, including a dictionary. Appropriate images from the CD include: 'Referee' and 'Torah'.

Presentation

If you pulled my shirt, not once, but twice, and you happened to be playing against me in a game of football, what do you think the referee might do?

Discuss the children's answers.

He might wave a yellow or red card and put my name in his little book.

Display and discuss the 'Referee' image from the CD at this point.

A referee's book is a special book.

Produce a large, heavy dictionary.

This isn't a referee's book – it wouldn't fit into the pocket of his shorts – but it is a special book. What is it used for?

Discuss the children's ideas again.

Here's another special book.

Repeat the process and discussion with two or three different books.

Produce a Bible.

Here is something completely different. What makes this book special is that it is a holy book, one that is treated with care and respect. There are all sorts of things inside it: history, poems, songs, miracles and stories. The second part tells us about the life of Jesus.

The Old Testament (the first part of the book) is one of my favourite sections, because it contains some wonderful stories. The Old Testament tells how, thousands of years ago, the Jews became a nation in what we now call the Middle East.

The young Jewish nation was rather like a child and had to learn how to live properly. So it created all sorts of laws about justice and mercy, and slavery and the family, that people today, the Jews included, would not tolerate. We have all grown up.

In the New Testament, Jesus shows us which are the most important laws of all. When Jesus was asked about the most important laws, he picked out: to love God and to love your neighbour as yourself (Matthew 22: 36–40). Neither of these two laws is in the Ten Commandments, but Jesus taught that they are the laws against which all others are to be measured. It's in this book!

You may want to discuss other religious books, such as the Torah.

Reflection or prayer

The Bible is a special book, a holy book. It teaches us the most important rules in life. May we grow in our understanding of these rules and learn to live our lives by the most important rule of all – the rule of love.

Lord of all things, above us and below, who created our world and all the laws which govern it, help us to love one another according to your law of love. Amen.

Alternative assembly topics
- A particular story from the Old Testament;
- The reason for laws;
- An aspect of the Sermon on the Mount (Matthew 5–7).

Development
- Take any one verse from the song 'Old Testament tales' and use it to create a storyboard.
- Investigate what other stories might be used to write more verses for the song.
- Create 'ten commandments' for the smooth running of a classroom, school or home. Make a list of as many different types of book that the children can think of.

Links
SEAL: New beginnings; Say no to bullying.
PSHE: 2b. To understand how and why rules and laws are made; **4a.** To try to see things from other points of view.

ASSEMBLIES

MORAL AND CHRISTIAN TEACHING

Shakespeare's water

Christian core

Christians not only give thanks for the world but also hold a duty of care in relation to it. Abuse and misuse of the world is an affront to God's creation so we are responsible for the impact we have upon it.

Other key ideas

In many areas of the world, the actions of human beings are having a detrimental affect upon the environment. The issue of climate change is important because, ultimately, the future of our species is at stake. It is in our own interest that we take the care of our environment seriously.

Music for assembling

Piotr Ilyich Tchaikovsky, *Romeo and Juliet*, 'Fantasy Overture' (approx 2' 30"; start after 9 minutes). (*Refer to Index for alternative suggestions.*)

Song on the CD

'Weeping clouds' was inspired by a visit to the Eden Project in Cornwall, where displays show the chain of events that link rainfall to the growth of plants. This song also includes a part for recorder.

See photocopiable pages 84 and 85.

Alternative music for singing

■ 'Water of life' by Christian Strover (*C&P*, 2) is an appropriate and well-expressed hymn.
■ Michael Saward's 'The Earth is yours, O God' (*C&P*, 6) is a simple, pretty and enchanting song.

Resources

A glass of water; appropriate images from the CD include: 'The Eden Project' and 'Drought'.

Presentation

Take a long and visible drink from the glass of water.

I had a drink like this once, when I was in London by the side of the river Thames where Shakespeare's theatre, the Globe, used to be. A man sitting on a seat nearby me interrupted me in a loud voice and said, 'You're drinking Shakespeare's water!'

I had to resist the urge to spit it out.

'What do you mean?' I asked, in a slightly worried voice. (Could I be arrested for drinking Shakespeare's water?)

'Shakespeare may have drunk that water 400 years ago', he insisted.

I thought, 'There are some strange people in London'.

As I am a polite person, I asked him how that could possibly be. He then gave me a detailed explanation of how the water cycle worked and how water went up to form clouds, fell as rain, was used by us, was then passed back to the rivers and seas to be taken up to form clouds, then fell again as rain … and so on. Round and round. Recycled forever. And that is how

SCHOLASTIC
www.scholastic.co.uk

Assemble and sing! For ages 7-11

Shakespeare's drink could conceivably have become my drink.

You can explain further if necessary.

At that point I threw away my water and bought an ice cream. Do you understand how the water cycle works?

Discuss the children's answers.

Plants, especially trees, play an important part in the water cycle, so we have to protect the world's forests and trees and use our water resources carefully.

You may want to discuss efforts being made to preserve trees and forests, and show 'The Eden Project' image from the CD here.

Water is vital for the future of life on Earth.

You could discuss here some drought-affected areas of the world, using the image of 'Drought' from the CD, or water use restrictions that are sometimes imposed even in 'wet' Britain.

Reflection or prayer

The future of the Earth is in our hands. If we don't look after the world, we will all suffer the consequences. There will be drought and hunger: the future will be bleak. Let us make sure that we all do our bit to ensure that this does not

happen and that the Earth has a bright and fertile future.

Dear God, your great creation is there for all to see and to enjoy. Bless those who work hard to preserve it for future generations. The world is full of a rich variety of animals and plants; make us care about these things enough to look after them properly so that we may enjoy them forever. Amen.

Alternative assembly topics

- Fair trade;
- Water Aid (see www.wateraid.org.uk);
- Planting trees for conservation (see www. woodland-trust.org.uk).

Development

- Investigate Christian Ecology. *What are its aims? What does it do?* (see www.christian-ecology.org.uk).
- Devise a 'recycling' plan for the school. *In what ways can school waste be reduced?*
- Draw a diagram showing the water cycle. Explain how it functions.
- Find out about climate change. *How many hard facts can you discover?*
- Find out about the Eden Project or visit it if you can (www.edenproject.com).

Links

SEAL: Changes (social skills).
PSHE: 1c. To face new challenges positively; 2h. To recognise the role of voluntary and pressure groups; 4a. To know that their actions affect themselves and others.

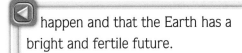

Beginnings

Christian core

The Bible begins with the words 'In the beginning'. Beginnings are important and Christians believe that when you start following the teachings of Jesus you are making a new beginning spiritually (John 3).

Other key ideas

Children often begin each school year with new teachers and classes. This can be challenging and even frightening for some. Such beginnings are also exciting, for they bring new experiences and opportunities to be seized.

Music for assembling

John Rutter, *Distant Land* (6' 10"). (*Refer to Index for alternative suggestions.*)

Song on the CD

'You're everywhere, wherever we go' is a very simple prayer asking for God's presence in all that we do. This song also includes parts for recorder.

See photocopiable pages 86 and 87.

Alternative music for singing

■ 'He's got the whole world in his hand', arranged by James Whitburn (*SOP*, 294; *C&P*, 19). You will need to sing this traditional spiritual with spirit.

■ 'When a knight won his spurs' by Jan Struther (*SOP*, 354; *WCV*, 66). Although this is a well-known favourite, it is still a fresh and stirring combination of words and music: 'Yet still to adventure … I ride'.

Resources

Appropriate images from the CD include: 'Beginning a journey', and 'Seedlings'.

Presentation

Start to tell a story:

To begin with, let's begin at the beginning. In the beginning, once upon a time, long ago and far away, before zebras got their stripes, when the world was young, at the start, long long ago, when time was young, in the very beginning (pause)… and they all lived happily ever after.

You may wish to pretend to move on to another part of the assembly.

Is something the matter? Did I forget to put my teeth in this morning?

Discuss what is missing and draw attention to the fact that you did remember something – the beginning.

Talk about beginnings, how important they are, how everything has to begin somewhere – great oaks from little

■SCHOLASTIC
www.scholastic.co.uk

Assemble and sing! For ages 7-11

acorns grow. *You may insert a story of a personal beginning of interest, or a story from current events in the news. For a more interactive assembly, get the children to tell of beginnings that they have enjoyed or beginnings that they dislike or fear – getting a new teacher, visiting the dentist and so on. You could start the discussion by displaying one of the images from the CD: 'Beginning a journey' or 'Seedlings'.*

However, like the assembly story this morning, beginnings are not enough. In our own lives, it is what we make of what comes next that is important.

You may end here, or link to current challenges in the children's lives, or to the problems faced by people beginning their lives again after a tsunami, war or famine.

Reflection or prayer

Dear Heavenly Father, life is full of beginnings. We pray for courage and determination to make the most of the opportunities that these new beginnings give us.

We pray for those facing difficult beginnings, those who struggle to make lives anew, perhaps after sad or tragic events. May they gain comfort and support from their friends and family and be given the strength to face up to whatever the future brings. Amen.

Alternative assembly topics
- Creation stories;
- Making new friends;
- New Year's Resolutions;
- Turning over a new leaf.

Development
- Compile 'tips for new teachers' – suggestions on how to make entry into a new class less terrifying for children.
- Write about an experience of coping with something new.
- Consider how the school might support charities that help other people rebuild their lives after some personal, man-made or natural disaster.

Links
SEAL: New beginnings; Going for goals; Changes.
PSHE: 1c. To face new challenges positively; **3a.** To know what makes a healthy lifestyle and how to make informed choices.

Endings

Christian core

Christians believe that God is in all things and is always with us, (Psalm 23). For Christians, death is the beginning of a time of eternal happiness with God (John 3: 16).

Other key ideas

■ Goodbyes are occasions of mixed emotions – of sadness and anticipation. They are also markers of change, of a future of unknown potential and excitement. The biggest goodbye is when someone dies. Even then, we can take time to reflect upon a life past and celebrate good memories that we have.

■ From the material below, you can construct an assembly for any 'ending' that you may have to deal with: the end of term; a special farewell for children leaving the school; teachers 'moving on' or a death that affects the school community.

Music for assembling

■ Farewell occasions can be very emotionally charged and you may take the view that no music, or something light, is called for.

■ Johann Sebastian Bach, Double Concerto in D minor for two violins and orchestra, BMV 1043, second movement, 'Largo ma non tanto' (2' 30" or more; full movement is 7' 42"). (Refer to Index for alternative suggestions.)

Song on the CD

'A blessing' should be sung prayerfully and may be used as an alternative to a spoken prayer.

See photocopiable pages 88 and 89.

Alternative music for singing

■ 'Lord of all hopefulness' by Jan Struther (WCV, 45; C&P, 52) and 'The Lord's my shepherd', based on Psalm 23 (WCV, 38 or C&P, 56 in a higher key and in a thinner setting), are both suitably comforting hymns.

■ Depending on the circumstances, you may wish to use a rousing hymn of praise such as 'Praise my soul the king of heaven' by Henry Francis Lyte (WCV, 18) or a specialist end-of-term hymn such as 'Lord dismiss us with thy blessing', by William Viner (WCV, 31).
A hymn of personal choice or the school hymn (if there is one) would suit.

Presentation

Sometimes, when I am reading a book, I can't wait to find out how it ends. I try not to, but I'm afraid I sometimes cheat. I turn to the last page to find out what happens in the end. Very often I find I need not have bothered because I guessed what was going to happen anyway.

Well, we have come here to face up to an ending today, one that we knew was coming, one that we had no need to look in the back of a book to find out about. Let us see if we can think of some of the best things that have happened during the past year(s).

If you are dealing with an end of year or similar, you can now talk to about all the events leading up to it – work, play, exams, friendships and so on.

SCHOLASTIC www.scholastic.co.uk

Assemble and sing! For ages 7-11

Now, as we come to this particular ending, I want you to take all those good memories with you, and look forward to the unknown and exciting days ahead in your new classes/schools.

In the event of a death, the assembly could be developed as follows:

Some endings are hard to face; they are often endings that we simply never expect. Here today we have to face up to the end of the life of someone who we knew and cared about.

You may want to elaborate here about the particular person's life.

We are fortunate to have shared some of our time on this Earth with _____. We can be grateful for their life and remember the good things about them.

You could discuss good memories the children have of the person, depending on the mood of the children.

Reflection or prayer

Go forth into the world in peace, be of good courage, hold fast to that which is good. And the blessing of God Almighty, the Father, the Son and the Holy Spirit, be with you and remain with you always. Amen.

If the occasion is the end of the year:

Dear Heavenly Father, we commend into your safekeeping all those who

are leaving here today. May they take away from this place useful lessons they have learned, friendships they have forged, and good memories they can cherish. May they delight in the challenges ahead of them and face the future with courage and humour. Let your blessing be upon them always.

If the occasion is a death:

We give grateful thanks for the life that we have been able to share with _____. Let us always remember, with joy in our hearts, all the good things about them. Heavenly Father, comfort all those who mourn the death of _____. May they take strength from the love and support of their friends and family and hope from your promises of love everlasting. Amen.

Alternative assembly topics

- Rites of passage;
- Celebrations: a christening; a marriage;
- Journeys and pilgrimages.

Development

Examine obituaries of a famous or historic person (choose with care) and then compose an obituary for the person that has died. You could use this strategy to help cope with a death in school.

Links

SEAL: Changes; New beginnings.
PSHE: 1c. To face new challenges positively;
2e. To reflect on spiritual issues.

Prayer matters

Christian core

The saying of prayers is a key part of Christian worship. Morning and evening prayers are said every day in large churches and cathedrals. Prayer is a personal way of communicating with God and you cannot force anyone to pray. In St Matthew's Gospel, the private nature of prayer is stressed and the exemplary nature of the Lord's Prayer explained (Matthew 6: 1–15).

Other key ideas

Prayer is a key feature of most community faiths. It is usually a way of reiterating faith and of communicating with God. Prayer is, for example, the second of the Five Pillars of Islam (salat). Judaism has its prayer rituals too, involving prayer shawls (tallit) and boxes of prayers (tefillin).

Music for assembling

Jules Massenet, *Thaïs*, 'Meditation' (4' 30"). (*Refer to Index for alternative suggestions.*)

Song on the CD

'The Lord's Prayer' is a modern setting based upon the version of the prayer given in the New English Bible, notable for characterising the devil as 'the evil one'.

See photocopiable pages 90 and 91.

Alternative music for singing

■ Some musical settings of the Lord's Prayer make considerable changes to the words, or do not comfortably match tune, rhythm and prayer. Both *WCV* and *C&P* contain alternative settings.

■ Donald Swann has set Mother Teresa's prayer to music (*C&P*, 94) or you could substitute a reverential hymn such as 'The Lord's my shepherd' (*WCV*, 38; *C&P*, 56).

Resources

Appropriate images from the CD include: 'Jewish prayer shawls', 'Muslims praying' and 'The Vatican'.

Presentation

This assembly starts with the presenter making a 'bit of a show' of themselves. Use an alternative approach if you are not comfortable with this.

I am the greatest! I am clever and smart, beautiful and talented. No one here has a brain as sharp as mine. I earn more money than all of you and I am so pleased that I am a much, much better person than any of you. I thank God for that!

Discuss with the children whether what you have just said sounds like a prayer. Ask them to explain their answers.

Being boastful like that is no way to make a prayer to God. A prayer is a way that people use to speak to God – it really is not the time to boast. You wouldn't talk to a friend like that, so you certainly shouldn't talk to God like that either.

But there were people who prayed

like that, who used to go to very public places, like street corners, and pray in loud, boastful tones so that everyone could hear them. Jesus wasn't very impressed when he saw people showing off like this. He made it pretty clear what he thought of them, but he also gave an example of the sort of prayer we should pray. This is written down in the Bible and we call it the Lord's Prayer.

You could read part of Matthew chapter 6 here, or let a child read the story out loud.

Jesus didn't say that you had to put your hands together, or kneel, or even shut your eyes when you pray, although people do this because they find that it helps them to pray. Can you suggest why?

Let the children give their own explanations.

When we talk to someone, we usually look them in the face but we can't do that when we talk to God, so people often do these things – such as closing their eyes – as a way of shutting out the world around them and concentrating on what they are saying.

You may also like to discuss the different ways that people pray. You could show the following images from the CD: 'Jewish prayer shawls', 'Muslims praying' and 'The Vatican'.

Reflection or prayer

Teach us, good Lord, how to pray. May we speak to you from our hearts and listen to your voice within.

Hear our prayer, O Lord.

Dear God, we try hard not to be boastful or selfish, but it is not easy. Help us when things become difficult. Help us to think of others and not always to put ourselves first.

Hear our prayer, O Lord.

Alternative assembly topics
■ Prayer rituals of other faiths;
■ Famous prayers: Mother Teresa's prayer;
■ Familiar prayers: grace before a meal; a benediction.

Development
■ *Why do Christians pray?* Discuss why people think prayer is important.
■ Make a collection of prayers said by famous people.
■ Examine the Lord's Prayer in several different forms. Let children compose a 'translation' in their own words.

Links
SEAL: Relationships (social skills).
PSHE: 4a. To care about other people's feelings; **2e.** To reflect on spiritual issues.

O praise God for the harvest

Words: *Paul Noble* **Music:** *Stuart Watkinson*

SCHOLASTIC
www.scholastic.co.uk

Assemble and sing! For ages 7-11

O praise God for the harvest

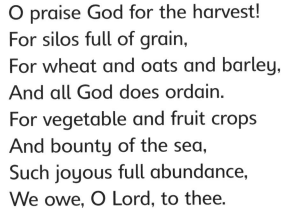

O praise God for the harvest!
For silos full of grain,
For wheat and oats and barley,
And all God does ordain.
For vegetable and fruit crops
And bounty of the sea,
Such joyous full abundance,
We owe, O Lord, to thee.

O praise God for the harvest!
For ploughmen and for ploughs,
For tractors and for combines,
For sheep and grazing cows.
The passage of the seasons,
The rain, the generous sun,
So sweet the touch of heaven,
On this our harvest won.

(Optional for harvest festival)

O praise God for the harvest!
By heaven's hand supplied,
The earth can yield sufficient
That none need be denied.
These offerings we bring you,
In poetry of praise,
To give our thanks for harvest,
And alleluias raise!

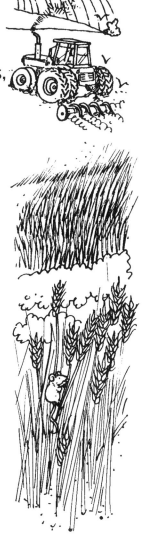

Assemble and sing! For ages 7-11

SCHOLASTIC
www.scholastic.co.uk

Children of your peace

Words: *Paul Noble* **Music:** *Stuart Watkinson*

SCHOLASTIC
www.scholastic.co.uk

Assemble and sing! For ages 7-11

Children of your peace

For countless acts of courage, of sacrifice and pain
Given for our freedom that all of us should gain
A world unbowed by violence, by force or evil whim;
Sing we thanks and offer, this remembrance hymn.

Not bounded by great mountains, by seas or deserts bare,
Held back not by oceans, or vastness of the air;
Each conflict scars the nations it ruins them with strife,
Dealing generations, death instead of life.

The sound of silent voices, still echoes in our ears,
Crying of the suffering, not faded by the years.
Our passion and desire must cause this folly cease:
Make us sons of quietness, children of your peace.

Born on a winter's night

Words: *Paul Noble* ***Music:*** *Stuart Watkinson*

Simply and not too fast ♩ = 100

Born on a win-ter's night__, Cra-dled__ by a__ mo-ther__ pure__,

intro to v. 1

Jes-us sav-iour__ of the__ world__, Wor-shipped on a__ sta- ble

end of v. 4   molto rit. . . . .

floor.   -joice.

Assemble and sing! For ages 7-11

Born on a winter's night

Born on a winter's night,
Cradled by a mother pure,
Jesus, saviour of the world,
Worshipped on a stable floor.

See, now the King of Kings,
Here on Earth, in ox's stall
Sleeping, yet he brings us hope,
Words of love and peace for all.

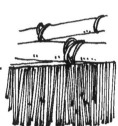

Sing out those songs of praise,
Lift your voices to the sky,
Celebrate Christ's birth on Earth.
Glory be to God on high!

Give thanks and praise the heavens!
Welcome the cries of baby's voice,
Every new life brings love and joy,
Let us all rejoice, rejoice!

■SCHOLASTIC
www.scholastic.co.uk

Bethlehem stills

Words: *Paul Noble* **Music:** *Stuart Watkinson*

Gently, with feeling

Soft through the trees the wind is sigh - ing, Sooth-ing the clouds in star - lit sky.___ Beth-le-hem stills, as Ma - ry, search - ing, Wants for a place her head___ to lie.___

melody

second part (optional)

Join - ing with voi - ces heav - en - ly

Join - ing with voi - ces heav - en - ly

sing - ing, Wel - come we now___ the Ho - ly child.

sing - ing, Wel - come we now the Ho - ly child.

Assemble and sing! For ages 7-11

Bethlehem stills

Soft through the trees the wind is sighing,
Soothing the clouds in starlit sky.
Bethlehem stills, as Mary, searching,
Wants for a place her head to lie.

Joining with voices heavenly singing,
Welcome we now the Holy Child.

Gentle on straw her head lies sleeping,
Warm in the byre, which beasts do share.
Bethlehem stills, as Mary, labouring,
Brings forth her babe in stable bare.

Chorus

Harsh is the hill where shepherds, guarding,
Hearken to angels from above.
Bethlehem stills, as shepherds wondering,
Kneel down and worship her sweet love.

Chorus

Bright is the dawn that now is breaking,
Turning the dark night into day.
Bethlehem stirs, and Mary, knowing,
Cradles the One who is the way.

Chorus

www.scholastic.co.uk

Easter hymn

Words: *Paul Noble* **Music:** *Stuart Watkinson*

Assemble and sing! For ages 7-11

Easter hymn

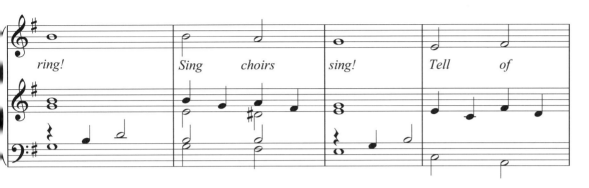

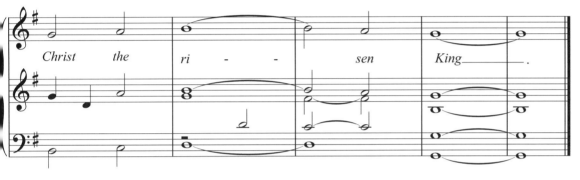

There is a story shall be told
Of darkness and of light,
Of our Lord's Easter sacrifice,
A victory of right.

> Ring bells ring!
> Christ is King!
> Joyful Easter bells do sing.
> Ring bells ring!
> Sing choirs sing!
> Tell of Christ the risen king.

For step by step and willingly
Our Lord his cross did bear,
He mounted cruel Golgotha's slopes
Each breath a plea, a prayer.

Chorus

'The will of God be done!' he cried,
His task on Earth complete,
He triumphed over death itself,
And evil did defeat.

Chorus

'Our Lord and Saviour is alive!'
All Christian people cry.
He lives within the hearts of men
Who worship him on high.

Chorus

Assemble and sing! For ages 7-11

Clap, clap your hands!

Words: Paul Noble **Music:** Stuart Watkinson (based on Psalm 47)

SCHOLASTIC
www.scholastic.co.uk

Assemble and sing! For ages 7-11

Clap, clap your hands!

Clap, clap your hands, with joy all ye people!
Voices and psalms be triumphant in praise.
Great is the king, who reigns over all things,
Mighty his works and most mighty his ways.

Shout, shout your praise, to God the Almighty!
Loud the acclaim be outpoured on his name.
His is the power beyond understanding,
Worship in awe and his glory proclaim.

Sing, sing your songs, in full adoration!
Praise in fine hymns, fill the air with the sounds.
Sing to the heights for all of creation,
Sing and be glad that his mercy abounds.

Assemble and sing! For ages 7-11

Creation song

Words: *Paul Noble* **Music:** *Stuart Watkinson*

SCHOLASTIC
www.scholastic.co.uk

Assemble and sing! For ages 7-11

Creation song

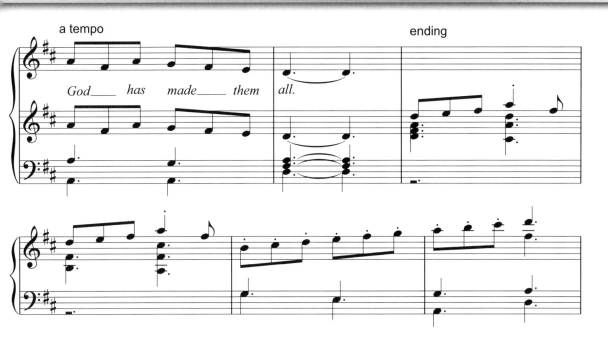

God___ has made___ them all.

For ambling aardvark and zany zho,
Give we thanks, O Lord,
For wand'ring whales wherever they go,
Give we thanks, O Lord.

Alleluia, Alleluia,
Alleluia, Alleluia,
List each creature from A to Z,
God has made them all.

For brawniest bear and sleepiest sloth,
Give we thanks, O Lord,
For secretive mouse in the undergrowth,
Give we thanks, O Lord.

Chorus

For cacophonous crow and silent snail,
Give we thanks, O Lord,
For spider monkey with gripping tail,
Give we thanks, O Lord.

Chorus

For dutiful dog and elusive eel,
Give we thanks, O Lord,
For patient heron with eye on a meal,
Give we thanks, O Lord.

Chorus

For evasive elk and comforting cat,
Give we thanks, O Lord,
For countless tadpoles the frog begat,
Give we thanks, O Lord.

Chorus

For lively lamb and dead dodo,
Give we thanks, O Lord,
For me, and all the creatures we
know,
Give we thanks, O Lord.

Chorus

**'Zho' is the name of a Tibetan cow; an alternative
spelling is 'zo'.*

Assemble and sing! For ages 7-11

Drink the laughing waters of life

Words: *Paul Noble* **Music:** *Stuart Watkinson*

SCHOLASTIC
www.scholastic.co.uk

Assemble and sing! For ages 7-11

Drink the laughing waters of life

ter, Drink the laugh - ing wa-ters of life.

ending

Laughter is the gift of an ever-loving
God,
Drink the laughing waters of life.
Laughter lights your eyes when you're
happy in your heart,
Drink the laughing waters of life.

Drink from life's fountain,
Drink the laughing waters of life.
Fill the world with laughter,
Drink the laughing waters of life.

Joyful is the sun as it beams down
from the sky,
Drink the laughing waters of life.
Joyful is the stream as it chuckles
going by,
Drink the laughing waters of life.

Chorus

Joyful is to smile as you come and as
you go,
Drink the laughing waters of life.
Joyful is to hug as you greet and say
hello,
Drink the laughing waters of life.

Chorus

Joyful is to care and to give
unbounded love,
Drink the laughing waters of life.
Joyful is the love that comes down
from God above,
Drink the laughing waters of life.

Chorus

Assemble and sing! For ages 7-11

SCHOLASTIC
www.scholastic.co.uk

SCORES AND LYRICS

CELEBRATION AND PRAISE

Good morning

Words: *Paul Noble* **Music:** *Stuart Watkinson*

SCHOLASTIC
www.scholastic.co.uk

Assemble and sing! For ages 7-11

Good morning

Good morning, welcoming sun,
Hello to joyful daybreak.
Welcome wind and welcome rain,
Blessings that all life sustain,
All are miracles that show
His world so beautiful below.

Good morning, welcoming sun,
Hello to all creation.
In the sky, in sea, on land,
Everywhere, on every hand,
Are God's miracles that show
His world so beautiful below.

Good morning, welcoming sun,
Hello to every person.
Brother, sister, stranger, friend,
Hands of fellowship extend,
Then mankind will truly know
How beautiful his world can grow.

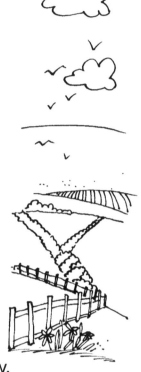

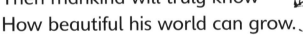

Assemble and sing! For ages 7-11

In the small things

Words: *Paul Noble* **Music:** *Stuart Watkinson*

SCHOLASTIC
www.scholastic.co.uk

Assemble and sing! For ages 7-11

In the small things

God of mighty cosmos, of wonders yet unknown,
We see you in the small things, there is heaven shown.
In luscious taste of autumn fruits,
In soaring gull that seaward swoops,
In flutter by of butterfly
And silver glint in twinkling eye,
We see you.
In the small things,
In the small things,
In the smallest things.

God of greatest ocean, of highest mountain known,
We see you in the small things, there is heaven shown.
In babbling brook that gentle flows,
In silent fall of winter snows,
In tender touch of baby's hand
And golden mat of sea-swept sand,
We see you.
In the small things,
In the small things,
In the smallest things.

God of tallest buildings, of concrete, brick and stone,
We see you in the small things, there is heaven shown.
In brittle shell of lowly snail,
In lazy swish of pony's tail,
In wind-blown corn that sways and bends
And happy smiles of playful friends,
We see you.
In the small things,
In the small things,
In the smallest things.

Shine!

Words: *Paul Noble* **Music:** *Stuart Watkinson*

SCHOLASTIC
www.scholastic.co.uk

Assemble and sing! For ages 7-11

Shine!

The light of the Lord shines on everyone,
The light of the Lord shines on everyone,
The light of the Lord shines on everyone,
Shine your light on me!

Shine, shine on everyone,
Shine your light on everyone,
Shine your light on ev'ryone,
Shine your light on me!

Come shine on the song and the singers too,
Come shine on the song and the singers too,
Come shine on the song and the singers too,
Shine your light on me!

Chorus

Come shine on my school and all my friends,
Come shine on my school and all my friends,
Come shine on my school and all my friends,
Shine your light on me!

Chorus

Come shine on the world, shine on everyone,
Come shine on the world, shine on everyone,
Come shine on the world, shine on everyone,
Shine your light on me!

Chorus

Assemble and sing! For ages 7-11

A good name

Words: *Paul Noble* ***Music:*** *Stuart Watkinson*

With movement ♩ = 88

Whe-ther you're an Os - car, a The - o or a Sean, Whe-ther you're a Char-lotte, O -

li - vi - a or Dawn, Whe-ther you're a Lu - cy, an Ell-ie or a Jen,

rit.

Whe-ther you're an Alf - ie, an Oll -y or a Ben: *Get your - self a good name, Like*

Car-ing, Kind or True: But you must earn a good___ name, A good name's up to___ you!

Assemble and sing! For ages 7-11

A good name

A good name is rather to be chosen than great riches.

Proverbs 22: 1

Whether you're an Oscar, a Theo or a Sean,
Whether you're a Charlotte, Olivia or Dawn,
Whether you're a Lucy, an Ellie or a Jen,
Whether you're an Alfie, an Olly or a Ben:

   Get yourself a good name,
   Like Caring, Kind or True:
   But you must earn a good name,
   A good name's up to you!

Whether you're a Sophie, an Annabelle or Mo,
Whether you're a David, a Joshua or Joe,
Whether you're an Andrew, an Adam or a Bill,
Whether you're an Esmé, a Lara or a Jill:

   Chorus

Whether you're an Emma, an Ali or a Kim,
Whether you're a Jacob, a Toby or a Tim,
Whether you're an Emily, a Jessica or Pam,
Whether you're a Daniel, a Nicholas or Sam:

   Chorus

SCHOLASTIC
www.scholastic.co.uk

God cares

Words: *Paul Noble* **Music:** *Stuart Watkinson*

Assemble and sing! For ages 7-11

God cares

Who cares for the lonely?
Living in a friendless world.
God cares for the lonely:
No one stands outside the love of God.

Who cares for the hungry?
Wanting for their daily bread.
God cares for the hungry:
No one stands outside the love of God.

Who cares for the homeless?
Seeking for a resting place.
God cares for the homeless:
No one stands outside the love of God.

Who cares for the suffering?
Bearing pain, or want, or grief.
God cares for the suffering:
No one stands outside the love of God.

Who cares for the caring?
Toiling through each day for love.
God cares for the caring:
No one stands outside the love of God.

Lord of dome and Lord of spire

Words: *Paul Noble* **Music:** *Stuart Watkinson*

Watch articulation ♩. = 76

Lord__ of dome and Lord of spire, Bo-th to heav'n-ly truth as-pire: But when faith and

doubt breed fear, Speak in each bel - iev-er's ear. Fill the spi - rit

and__ the mind With__ the love__ of all man - kind__ .

Lord of dome and Lord of spire

Lord of dome and Lord of spire,
Both to heav'nly truth aspire:
But when faith and doubt breed fear,
Speak in each believer's ear.
Fill the spirit and the mind
With the love of all mankind.

Lord of different, Lord of same,
Who did share our Earthly frame:
What the colour, wit or size,
All are precious in your eyes.
Let our spirits now unite,
In your truth and in your light.

Lord of music, Lord of dance,
Which great gifts our lives enhance,
Charge each rhythm, beat and song,
Push the pulse of life along.
Fire our spirits as we sing
And we'll make the heavens ring.

SCHOLASTIC
www.scholastic.co.uk

Love your neighbour

Words: *Paul Noble* **Music:** *Stuart Watkinson*

SCHOLASTIC
www.scholastic.co.uk

Assemble and sing! For ages 7-11

Love your neighbour

Love your neighbour as yourself,
Christ Jesus made this plea,
And charged us this command to keep:
The gift of love is free,
The gift of love is free.

Love your neighbour as yourself,
Whoever he may be,
Whatever race, or age, or creed:
The gift of love is free,
The gift of love is free.

Love your neighbour as yourself,
For action is a key
That opens up each caring heart:
The gift of love is free,
The gift of love is free.

Love your neighbour as yourself,
God loves, and so must we.
All Christians now must do their part:
The gift of love is free,
The gift of love is free.

No greater thing

Words: *Paul Noble* **Music:** *Stuart Watkinson*

Keep moving ♩ = 84

Jet planes skate the sky - line,__ Ships search the seas be - low. But hope came down from hea - ven,__ There's no grea - ter thing I know.

ending

■SCHOLASTIC
www.scholastic.co.uk

Assemble and sing! For ages 7-11

No greater thing

Jet planes skate the skyline,
Ships search the seas below,
But hope came down from heaven,
There's no greater thing I know.

Unseen, all around us,
Fly words our mouths dismiss,
But truth came down from heaven,
There's no greater thing than this.

Vaccines, pills and potions,
Bid all our suffering cease,
But love came down from heaven,
There's no greater thing than this.

Stars peer through the ages,
The sun gives Earth its bliss,
But Christ came down from heaven,
There's no greater thing than this.

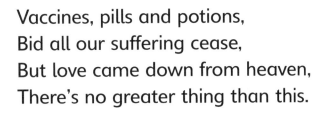

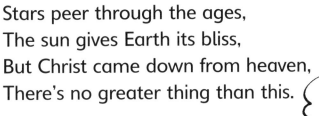

Old Testament tales

Words: *Paul Noble* **Music:** *Stuart Watkinson*

SCHOLASTIC
www.scholastic.co.uk

Assemble and sing! For ages 7-11

Old Testament tales

Genesis begins the story,
Heav'n and Earth were formed in glory.
God was might, his words held sway,
They divided night from day.

Psalms and prophets, priests and kings,
Myths and tales of wondrous things.

Life was breathed on God's creations,
Tigers, toads and our relations.
Adam roamed o'er Eden's land –
Eve was there to hold his hand.

Chorus

Serpent showed them good and evil,
Caused a really great upheaval.
Cain, their wicked wayward son,
Murdered their more able one.

Chorus

'Look', said God, 'all flesh's corrupted.'
'Build a boat!' he then instructed.
Creatures crowded on Noah's ark,
Roar and squeak and moo and bark.

Chorus

Babel's tower left all gaping,
Climbing high, it went sky-scraping.
Down it fell, so ran the rabble,
Speaking only Babel's babble.

Chorus

Trusting father did not falter,
By the sacrificial altar.
Isaac, son of Abraham,
Gave his place up to a ram.

Chorus

Joseph ended up in slavery,
Sold by brothers most unsavoury.
He was dressed in cloth of note –
Splendid rainbow-coloured coat.

Chorus

Brothers made up, then they parted,
Then the twelve new tribes got
    started.
Moses set his people free,
Making paths across the sea.

Chorus

Long before the phone and text,
Scribes wrote down what happened
    next.
They set down an ancient tale –
History of Israel.

Chorus

Weeping clouds

Words: *Paul Noble* **Music:** *Stuart Watkinson*

SCHOLASTIC
www.scholastic.co.uk

Assemble and sing! For ages 7-11

Weeping clouds

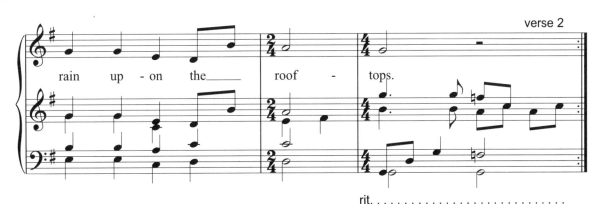

verse 2

rain up - on the____ roof - tops.

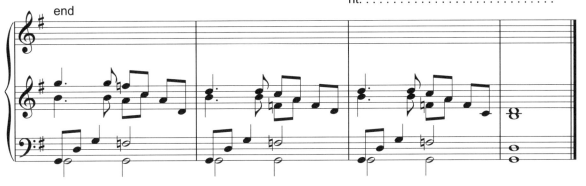

rit. . . . .

end

Roots drink from the fertile soil,
Where the rain has fallen.
Plants enjoy this heav'nly gift:
Food for Eden's garden.
Leaves which breathe to cloud the sky
Fill the air with raindrops.
Weeping clouds cry happy tears
Of rain upon the rooftops.

When each cloud no rain can cry,
When each leaf stops breathing,
Then will roots no longer drink,
Then will crops start ailing.
God gives us his world in trust,
Beauty that's for sharing.
In our hands the future rests.
Make now the time for caring.

Assemble and sing! For ages 7-11

You're everywhere, wherever we go

Words: *Paul Noble* **Music:** *Stuart Watkinson*

SCHOLASTIC
www.scholastic.co.uk

Assemble and sing! For ages 7-11

You're everywhere, wherever we go

Each day, O Lord,
We try to do
The best we can,
Our work for you.
You're ev'rywhere,
Wherever we go.
Please hold us in your hand.

And when at times
It is hard to know
What is right and true,
It's then you show
You're ev'rywhere,
Wherever we go
And hold us in your hand.

O Lord, our God,
We may be small
But you know and guard us,
Love us all,
Come ev'rywhere,
Wherever we go,
And hold us in your hand.

A blessing

Words: *Paul Noble* ***Music:*** *Stuart Watkinson*

SCHOLASTIC
www.scholastic.co.uk

Assemble and sing! For ages 7-11

A blessing

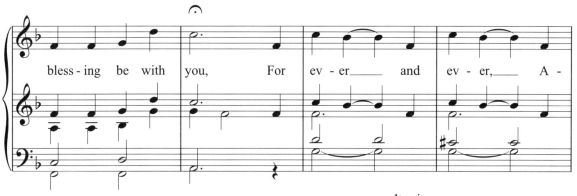

bless - ing   be with   you,   For   ev - er____ and   ev - er,____   A -

molto rit. . . . .
second part (optional)

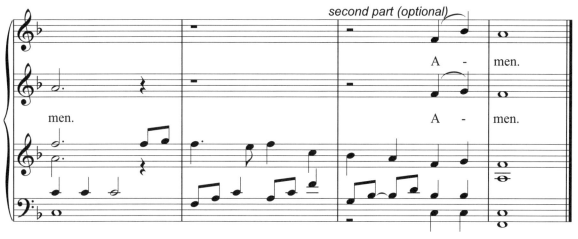

men.   A -   men.

                                                                          A -   men.

As you go,
May the Lord go with you,
Wherever life's journey may direct.
May God hold you and protect you,
And wrap you forever in his arms.
May you walk 'neath the wings of angels,
In the light of his glory and grace.
And his blessing be with you,
For ever and ever, Amen.
Amen.

SCHOLASTIC
www.scholastic.co.uk

The Lord's Prayer

Words: *The New English Bible* ***Music:*** *Stuart Watkinson*

SCHOLASTIC
www.scholastic.co.uk

Assemble and sing! For ages 7-11

The Lord's Prayer

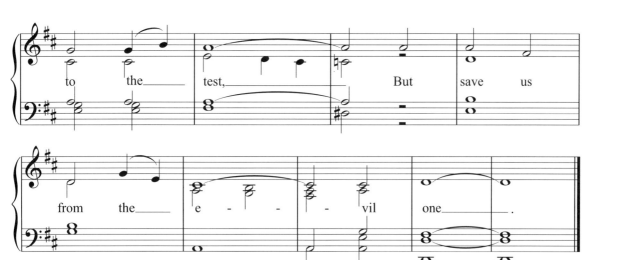

Our Father in heaven,
Thy name be hallowed;
Thy kingdom come,
Thy will be done,
On Earth as is in heaven.
Give us this day our daily bread.
Forgive us the wrong we have done,
As we have forgiven those who have wronged us.
And do not bring us to the test,
But save us from the evil one.

Music for assembling

The following selection is an introduction to suitable music for assembling. The extracts have been listed in alphabetical order, by composer, with the page number of the assembly for which the extract might be particularly suitable, given in brackets alongside.

Approximate timings of the extracts are given in minutes and seconds; precise timings will depend on the tempo of the recording used. The length of the extract is, of course, a matter of choice.

The title of the assembling music ought to be displayed and children can be encouraged in their listening by being told what they might listen for, be it a particular instrument, motif or sound.

Babell, William,
▷ Concerto for descant recorder, Op. 3 No. 1, 'Allegro' (1'20")
A spirited and tuneful eighteenth-century piece played on an instrument which will be familiar to children but with a degree of musical skill that will surprise them. [p.36]

Bach, Johann Sebastian,
▷ *Brandenburg Concerto* No. 4 in G Major, BWV 1049, 'Allegro' (4'02")
Something a little more demanding for children to listen to. [p.26]
▷ *Christmas Oratorio*, 'Nun seid ihr wohl gerochen' (3'15")
For cheerful, upbeat Christmas music, there is little to rival the trumpets in the final chorus – arranged for brass ensemble. [p.14]
▷ *Jesu, Joy of Man's Desiring*, BMV 147, arranged for orchestra (3'12")

A moving and tranquil tune [p.16]
▷ *Sheep May Safely Graze*, Cantata No. 208, BMV 208 (4'57")
This radiates pastoral tranquillity, as was intended. [p.18]
▷ *Air on a G String*, from Suite No. 3, BWV 1068 (3'10")
Slow and smoothly beautiful. [p.26]
▷ Double Concerto in D minor for two violins and orchestra, BMV 1043, second movement, 'Largo ma non tanto' (2'30" or more; full movement 7'42")
One of Bach's masterpieces, intense and sublimely beautiful. [p.46]

Barber, Samuel,
▷ Adagio for strings (3'40")
A beautiful melody; it may be too slow and agonisingly sad for some tastes. [p.16]

Brahms, Johannes,
▷ Violin Concerto in D minor, Op. 77, second movement, 'Adagio' (3'30")
Brahms thought this Adagio to be feeble but this is not the judgement of history. [p.28]

Crusell, Bernhard,
▷ Concerto No. 2 for clarinet and orchestra, Op. 5, third movement, 'Rondo' (96'00")
Crusell was having a humorous moment when he added the loud chords to the chirpy third movement. [p.22]

Debussy, Claude,
▷ *The Children's Corner*, 'Golliwog's Cakewalk' (2'53")
A cheerful piece, dedicated by Debussy, to his improbably named young daughter 'Chouchou'. [p.22]

Delius, Frederick,
▷ *La Calinda* (4'32")
This cheerful, celebratory piece has the added attraction of a tambourine accompaniment. [p.12]
▷ *To be Sung on a Summer Night on the Water 1* (2'16")
Vocal pieces are rarely appropriate for assembly 'mood' music, but the wordless performance of this piece by the Cambridge Singers is beautiful, haunting and tuneful. [p.8]

Dvořák, Antonin,
▷ Symphony No. 9 in E minor, Op. 95 (from the *New World*), 'Largo' (2'35")
The evocative opening few minutes of the second movement are beloved by advertisers, and probably need no introduction. [p.36]
▷ *Slavonic Dance in G minor*, Op. 46 No. 8 (4'01")
There is nothing shy and retiring about Dvořák's joyful and boisterous musical celebration. [p.38]

Elgar, Edward,
▷ *Chanson de Matin*, Op. 15 No. 2 (3'02")
Typically Elgar, this expansive theme is a fine wake-up call and a tune to stretch to. [p.24]
▷ Variations on an Original Theme *(Enigma)*, Op. 36 No. 9, 'Nimrod' (4'11")
This tune is played annually at the Cenotaph Service of Remembrance. It is Elgar's affectionate recollection of a friend's conversation on a summer's evening. [p.10, 46]

Finzi, Gerald,
▷ *Severn Rhapsody* (3'00" or more)

Assemble and sing! For ages 7-11

Here Finzi, an English composer, paints a musical picture of the hills and meandering waters of a beautiful corner of England. [p.8]

Goodall, Howard,
▷ *23rd Psalm, The Lord is My Shepherd* (2'42")
Children may well be familiar with Howard Goodall's setting of the 23rd Psalm as it is used as the signature tune for the *The Vicar of Dibley* TV series. [p.18]

Grieg, Edvard,
▷ *Peer Gynt Suite*, Op. 46 No. 1, 'Morning Mood' (4'32")
With its familiar undulating tune, this is wonderfully evocative of sunrise. [p.24]
▷ *Holberg Suite*, 'Praeludium' (2'32")
Grieg has produced a strong melody, full of anticipation. [p.40]

Handel, George Frederick,
▷ Concerto for orchestra and organ in F Major, HWV 295, *The Cuckoo and the Nightingale*, second movement, 'Allegro' (3'32")
Wonderful combinations of different sounds; the children will enjoy listening for the cuckoo. [p.34]
▷ Concerto Grosso, Op. 3 No. 2, 'Largo' (2'33")
A gentle and classically wistful piece from Handel. [p.42]
▷ *Water Music*, Suite No. 2, 'Hornpipe' (3'37")
A comfortable and, to most adults, familiar piece. [p.44]

Haydn, Joseph,
▷ Trumpet Concerto in E flat major, 'Andante' (3'47")

A slow and somewhat sombre composition with rich, resonating trumpet sounds. [p.32]

Hely-Hutchinson, Victor,
▷ A Carol Symphony, first movement, 'Allegro energetico' (4'11")
A splendid bouncy variation on a well-known carol. [p.14]

Khachaturian, Aram,
▷ *Spartacus*, 'Adagio of Spartacus and Phrygia' (first three minutes only)
This will send broad swathes of all-encompassing orchestral sound echoing around the hall. [p.34]

Massenet, Jules,
▷ *Thaïs*, 'Meditation' (4'30")
Composed as an orchestral interlude for his opera, it is a smooth, beguiling tune. [p.46, 48]

Mozart, Leopold, *(father of Wolfgang Amadeus)*
▷ *Toy Symphony*, 'Allegro' (4'28")
This charming symphony uses a wide range of percussion noises – plenty for the children to listen for here, although you need to fade out before the end if you don't wish to hear the cuckoo getting shot. [p.30]

Mozart, Wolfgang Amadeus,
▷ Concerto in C for flute, harp and orchestra, KV299, 'Andantino' (4'06")
Gentle yet cheerfully tuneful and upbeat. [p.18]
▷ Quintet for clarinet and string quartet in A Major, 'Allegro' (4'05")

A rich textured, cheerful piece. [p.30]
▷ Sonata for two pianos in D major, K448, 'Andante' (3'10")
A few years ago, research suggested that listening to music when a baby causes one's intelligence to be improved. This piece was thought best for the purpose. Play the Andante and grow brains at the same time. [p.28]
▷ *Eine Kleine Nachtmusik*, K525, 'Rondo: Allegro' (5'17")
The 'night music' may be a bit of a musical cliché but it still has tunes to be reckoned with. [p.32]
▷ Clarinet concerto in A major, first movement (3'42")
The cheerful introductory section is spirited and easy on the ear. [p.38]

Poulenc, Francis,
▷ Concerto for piano, 'Allegretto' (3'45")
Something different, an entertaining piece of musical froth written for an American tour. [p.32]

Prokofiev, Sergei,
▷ *Lieutenant Kijé Suite*, Op. 60, 'Troika' (2'57")
Complete with sleigh bells and excited piccolo; very Christmassy. [p.12]

Purcell, Henry,
▷ *Abdelazer*, 'Rondo' (1'34")
One of the greatest British composers produced this tune that was used by another, Benjamin Britten, in the Young Person's Guide to the Orchestra. If the 'Rondo' is too short for you, you could use a Britten extract instead. [p.38]

continued

SCHOLASTIC
www.scholastic.co.uk

◀ continued

Rachmaninov, Serge,
▷ Rhapsody on a Theme of Paganini (first 3'15" or 3 minutes from 15'30")
Spirited wake-up-and-take-notice music is provided by the dancing notes of the piano in the opening variation. The later extract has the big picture sound of unrestrained passion and romance. [p.48]

Rimsky-Korsakov,
▷ Nikolai, Scheherazade, 'The Tale of the Kalender Prince' (3'20")
This is a fine, dreamy introduction for any storyteller. [p.40]

Rodrigo, Joaquin,
▷ Concierto de Aranjuez for guitar and orchestra, second movement, 'Adagio' (3'20")
With a slight melancholy edge, this concerto has a melody overlaid with the lingering tones of the cor anglais. [p.16]

Rutter, John,
▷ Distant Land (6'10")
This is an orchestral version of a choral work written in 1991 that was inspired by the release of Nelson Mandela from prison; a sweeping, lyrical composition. [p.44]
▷ Nativity Carol (4'50")
A hauntingly beautiful modern classic. [p.14]
▷ Requiem Mass: Pie Jesu (3'30")
Words can be a distraction for children settling down for an 'act of worship', but it is worth making an exception for this modern setting of the Requiem Mass sung in Latin. [p.10]

Saint-Saëns, Camille,
▷ Carnival of the Animals

This is an excellent source for animal music. Both 'The Aquarium' (2'31") and 'The Swan' (2'47") are slow and soothing, but if you wish to agitate your children a little, they could march in to 'The Royal March of the Lion' (2'16"). [p.20]

Schubert, Franz,
▷ Symphony No. 3 in D (D 200), second movement, 'Allegretto' (4'39")
A pretty, staccato tune. [p.30]

Shostakovich, Dmitri,
▷ Concerto No. 2 for piano and orchestra, Op. 102, 'Andante' (2'48")
One of Shostakovich's most popular tunes, enchanting and dreamy, and well worth a good listen. [p.36]

Sibelius, Jean,
▷ Karelia Suite, Op. 11 (3'51")
The opening few minutes are cumulatively stirring and brassy. [p.44]

Strauss, Richard,
▷ Horn Concerto No. 1 in E flat, Op. 11, third movement, 'Rondo' (4'57")
Difficult to play but easy on the ear, this deserves to be more widely known. [p.22]

Tchaikovsky, Piotr Ilyich,
▷ The Nutcracker Suite, Op. 71a, 'Miniature Overture' (3'13")
This will provide a joyful upbeat start to an assembly. [p.26]
▷ Symphony No. 5 in E minor, second movement, 'Andante cantabile' (3'00")
This is smooth and gentle, although it becomes more rousing after about three

minutes. [p.28]
▷ Romeo and Juliet, 'Fantasy Overture' (approx 2'30"; start after 9' minutes)
As would be expected, this is full of a sense of impending tragedy. [p.42]

Telemann, Georg Philipp,
▷ Overture in F major (Alster Overture, 'Concert of Frogs and Crows') (3'18")
Somewhat unsettling (and breaking the rules about calm assembling music), the clashing and amusing sounds created by Telemann are different! [p.20]

Vaughan-Williams, Ralph,
▷ Fantasia on Greensleeves (3'09")
A familiar pastoral tune tinged with sadness. [p.8]
▷ 5 Variants of Dives and Lazarus (3'30")
This is the sort of tuneful pastoral air of which the composer is master. [p.42]

Walton, William,
▷ Henry V Suite, 'Passacaglia: The Death of Falstaff' (2'47")
A strong, atmospheric piece, sombre as befits a serious subject. [p.10]

Warlock, Peter,
▷ Capriol Suite, 'Pieds-en-l'air' (2'34")
This extract has the smooth, dreamy feel of a lullaby. Indeed, another modern British composer, John Rutter, has written a carol (Christmas Night, Carols for Choirs, OUP, No. 78) to this tune. [p.12]

Picture resources

The following images are all available on the CD-ROM:

Occasions
Aum
Bethlehem conflict
Bethlehem dividing wall
Birthday party
Effingham Cross
Field of poppies
Harvest festival
Islamic crescent
Khanda
Menorah
Mother and baby
Somme cemetery
Star of David

Celebration and praise
Baby's hand
Butterfly
Clowns

Diwali
Elephant
Greetings
Ladies laughing
Ocean
Otter
People singing
Porcupine
Robin
Shepherd
Sunrise
Terrapin
The Light of the World, by
Holman Hunt

Moral and Christian teaching
Beginning a journey
Camels
Cathedral

Church
Crow
Dennis the Menace
Drought
Intercity train
Monkeys
Mosque
Paramedics
Rabbit
Referee
Seedlings
Synagogue
The Eden Project
The Red Cross
Torah

Reflection
Jewish prayer shawls
Muslims praying
The Vatican